BRIGHT & Brainy

4th Grade Practice

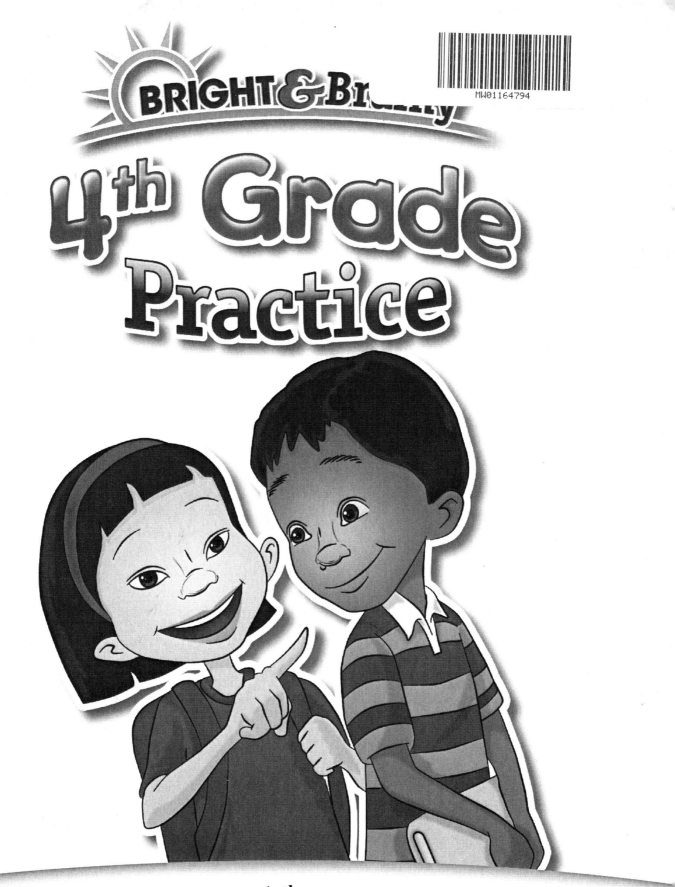

Author

Christine Dugan, M.A.Ed.

SHELL EDUCATION

Publishing Credits

Dona Herweck Rice, *Editor-in-Chief*; Robin Erickson, *Production Director*;
Lee Aucoin, *Creative Director*; Timothy J. Bradley, *Illustration Manager*;
Sara Johnson, M.S.Ed, *Senior Editor*; Evelyn Garcia, *Associate Education Editor*;
Leah Quillian, *Assistant Editor*; Grace Alba, *Designer*;
Corinne Burton, M.A.Ed., *Publisher*

Standard

© 2010 National Governors Association Center for Best Practices and Council of Chief State School Officers (CCSS)

Shell Education

5301 Oceanus Drive
Huntington Beach, CA 92649-1030
http://www.shelleducation.com

ISBN 978-1-4258-0908-9

© 2012 Shell Educational Publishing, Inc.
Reprinted 2013

Table of Contents

Introduction 4

How to Use This Book 6

Correlation to Standards 8

Language Arts Activity Pages 11

    Reading: Foundational Skills 11

    Language Conventions 15

    Reading: Informational Text 57

    Vocabulary Acquisition and Use 94

    Reading: Literature 113

    Fluency 142

    Writing 144

    Speaking and Listening 148

Mathematics Activity Pages 150

    Operations and Algebraic Thinking 150

    Number and Operations in Base Ten 166

    Number and Operations—Fractions 197

    Measurement and Data 224

    Geometry 241

References Cited 249

Answer Key 250

Contents of the Resource CD 272

Every Child Is Bright and Brainy

The Need for Continual Practice

"Practice makes perfect."

That's what they say, and it's usually true! Although educational practices have changed over time, some key methods have stayed the same. Children need plenty of opportunity to practice skills and show what they know. The more they do, the more they can transfer their learning to everyday life—and future success!

Of course, there has to be a good purpose for the practice. That is where the pages in this book come in. Created with the essential standards in mind, each activity page focuses on a particular concept, skill, or skill-set and provides students abundant opportunities to practice and achieve mastery.

Annis and Annis (1987) found that continual repetition helps increase the levels of the Bloom cognitive domain. In other words, practice helps students learn in a wide variety of ways at all levels of cognitive ability. It provides students opportunities to think more deeply about the subjects they are studying. Marzano (2010) asserts that in order for students to independently display their learning, it is necessary for them to practice procedural skills. Providing students with ample opportunity to practice remains a key strategy for employing the best educational practices in or out of the classroom.

Every Child Is Bright and Brainy (cont.)

Understanding the Standards

The Common Core State Standards were developed in collaboration with a wide variety of educators through the Common Core State Standards Initiative. The goal was to create a clear and consistent framework to prepare students for higher education and the workforce. To this end, teachers, school administrators, and other educational experts worked together in a state-led effort coordinated by the National Governors Association Center for Best Practices (NGA) and the Council of Chief State School Officers (CCSSO).

The standards incorporate the most effective models from around the country and around the globe, providing teachers and parents with a shared understanding of what students are expected to learn. The consistency of the standards provides a common, appropriate benchmark for students unrelated to their location.

According to the NGA and the CCSSO, these standards meet the following criteria:

☼ They are aligned with college and work expectations;

☼ They are clear, understandable, and consistent;

☼ They include rigorous content and application of knowledge through high-order skills;

☼ They build upon strengths and lessons of current state standards;

☼ They are informed by other top-performing countries so that all students are prepared to succeed in our global economy and society; and

☼ They are evidence-based

Students who meet these standards within their K–12 education should have the skills and knowledge necessary to succeed in their educational careers and beyond.

Making It Work

It is important for you to understand the key features of this book, so that you can use it in a way that works for you and your students.

- **Standards-based practice.** The exercises in *Bright & Brainy: 4th Grade Practice* are aligned with the Common Core State Standards. Each activity page focuses on a particular concept, skill, or skill-set and provides students ample opportunities to practice and achieve mastery.

- **Clear, easy-to-understand activities.** The exercises in this book are written in a kid-friendly style.

- **Assessment of student progress.** Based on student progress, the Common Core State Standards Correlation Chart (pages 9–10) helps identify the grade-level standards with which students may need additional support.

- **Reinforcement of key grade-level concepts.** Each activity provides practice of key grade-level language arts and mathematics skills in an organized and meaningful way.

- **Stand-alone activity pages.** Each activity is flexible and can be used independently in a variety of instructional or at-home settings.

The chart below provides suggestions for how to implement the activities.

Whole/Small Group	Individual	At Home/Homework
• Read and discuss the directions at the beginning of each activity. Work practice problems on an interactive whiteboard, document camera, or other display method. • Have students work problems on the interactive whiteboard. • Have students take turns reading each question. • Display the problems and review and correct them. • Read and discuss responses.	• Create folders for each student. Include a copy of their selected activity pages. • Collect work and check student answers, or provide each student with copies of the answer key and allow them to check their own work. • Select specific activity pages to support individual students' needs for additional practice.	• Provide each student with activity pages to reinforce skills. • Collect work and check student answers, or provide each student with copies of the answer key and allow them to check their own work. • Select specific activity pages to provide extra support in areas where individual students may need additional practice.

Making It Work (cont.)

Bright & Brainy: 4th Grade Practice provides practice pages for a broad range of Common Core language arts and mathematics standards. Language arts topics are designed to provide students practice in the most vital skills included in the Common Core Standards. These range from reading foundational skills to fluency, and from writing to speaking and listening. Activities designed to support student learning of how to read informational texts, literature, and vocabulary skills round out the carefully chosen exercises. Within each of these broad areas are individual activity pages centering on subtopics, such as letter recognition, alike and different, antonyms, and rhyming. Each covered skill is crucial to achieving language fluency and to setting the stage for future success in language arts. Likewise, the chosen mathematics skills represent fundamental and integral topics from the Common Core Standards. Clear, student-friendly exercises center around the essential areas of counting and cardinal numbers, number and operations in base ten, operations and algebraic thinking, measuring, data, and geometry.

Individual lessons engage students in mastering specific skills, including more, less, same, sequencing, alike and different, and flat vs. solid.

This book covers the following:

- Reading: Foundational Skills
- Language Conventions
- Reading: Informational Text
- Vocabulary Acquisition and Use
- Reading: Literature
- Fluency
- Writing
- Speaking and Listening
- Operations and Algebraic Thinking
- Number and Operations in Base Ten
- Measurement and Data
- Geometry

Additionally, the Resource CD allows for easy access to the student activity pages in this book. Electronic PDF files of all the activity pages are included on the CD.

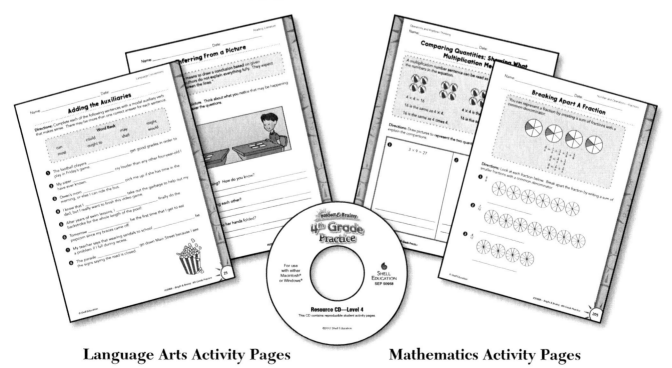

Language Arts Activity Pages   **Mathematics Activity Pages**

Correlation to Standards

Shell Education is committed to producing educational materials that are research and standards based. In this effort, we have correlated all of our products to the academic standards of all 50 United States, the District of Columbia, the Department of Defense Dependent Schools, and all Canadian provinces. We have also correlated to the Common Core State Standards.

How to Find Standards Correlations

To print a customized correlation report of this product for your state, visit our website at **http://www.shelleducation.com** and follow the on-screen directions. If you require assistance in printing correlation reports, please contact Customer Service at 1-800-858-7339.

Purpose and Intent of Standards

Legislation mandates that all states adopt academic standards that identify the skills students will learn in kindergarten through grade twelve. Many states also have standards for Pre-K. This same legislation sets requirements to ensure the standards are detailed and comprehensive.

Standards are designed to focus instruction and guide adoption of curricula. Standards are statements that describe the criteria necessary for students to meet specific academic goals. They define the knowledge, skills, and content students should acquire at each level. Standards are also used to develop standardized tests to evaluate students' academic progress.

Teachers are required to demonstrate how their lessons meet state standards. State standards are used in development of all of our products, so educators can be assured they meet the academic requirements of each state.

Common Core State Standards

The lessons in this book are aligned to the Common Core State Standards (CCSS). The standards listed on pages 9–10 support the objectives presented throughout the lessons.

Common Core State Standards Correlation Chart

Language Arts	
Reading: Foundational Skills	**Page(s)**
RF.4.3—Know and apply grade-level phonics and word analysis skills in decoding words	11–14
Language Conventions	**Page(s)**
L.4.1—Use relative pronouns and relative adverbs	15–20
L.4.1—Form and use the progressive verb tenses	21–23
L.4.1—Use modal auxiliaries to convey various conditions	24–25
L.4.1—Order adjectives within sentences according to conventional patterns	26–28
L.4.1—Form and use prepositional phrases	29–31
L.4.1—Produce complete sentences, recognizing and correcting inappropriate fragments and run-ons	32–34
L.4.1—Correctly use frequently confused words	35–37
L.4.2—Use correct capitalization	38–40
L.4.2—Use commas and quotation marks to mark direct speech and quotations from a text	41–42
L.4.2—Use a comma before a coordinating conjunction in a compound sentence	43–44
L.4.2—Spell grade-appropriate words correctly, consulting references as needed	45–46
L.4.3—Choose words and phrases to convey ideas precisely	47–50
L.4.3—Choose punctuation for effect	51–54
L.4.3—Differentiate between contexts that call for formal English and situations where informal discourse is appropriate	55–56
Reading: Informational Text	**Page(s)**
RI.4.1—Refer to details and examples in a text when explaining what the text says explicitly and when drawing inferences from the text	57–58
RI.4.2—Determine the main idea of a text and explain how it is supported by key details; summarize the text	59–65
RI.4.3—Explain events, procedures, ideas, or concepts in a historical, scientific, or technical text	66–69
RI.4.5—Describe the overall structure of events, ideas, concepts, or information in a text or part of a text	70–72
RI.4.6—Compare and contrast a firsthand and secondhand account of the same event or topic; describe the differences in focus and the information provided	73–81
RI.4.7—Interpret information presented visually, orally, or quantitatively and explain how the information contributes to an understanding of the text in which it appears	82–90
RI.4.8—Explain how an author uses reasons and evidence to support particular points in a text	91–93
Vocabulary Acquisition and Use	**Page(s)**
L.4.4—Use context as a clue to the meaning of a word or phrase	94–97
L.4.4—Use common, grade-appropriate Greek and Latin affixes and roots as clues to the meaning of a word	98–101
L.4.4—Consult reference materials, both print and digital, to find the pronunciation and determine or clarify the precise meaning of key words and phrases	102–104
L.4.5—Explain the meaning of simple similes and metaphors	105–108
L.4.5—Recognize and explain the meaning of common idioms, adages, and proverbs	109–112
Reading: Literature	**Page(s)**
RL.4.1—Refer to details and examples in a text when explaining what the text says explicitly and when drawing inferences from the text	113–117
RL.4.2—Determine a theme of a story, drama, or poem from details in the text; summarize the text	118–121
RL.4.3—Describe in depth a character, setting, or event in a story or drama, drawing on specific details in the text	122–130
RL.4.4—Determine the meaning of words and phrases as they are used in a text	131–134
RL.4.6—Compare and contrast the point of view from which different stories are narrated	135–141
Fluency	**Page(s)**
RF.4.4—Read with sufficient accuracy and fluency to support comprehension	142–143

Common Core State Standards Correlation Chart *(cont.)*

Language Arts (cont.)	
Writing (cont.)	**Page(s)**
W.4.1—Write opinion pieces on topics or texts, supporting a point of view with reasons and information	144–147
Speaking and Listening	**Page(s)**
SL.4.1—Engage effectively in a range of collaborative discussions	148–149
Mathematics	
Operations and Algebraic Thinking	**Page(s)**
4.OA.1—Interpret a multiplication equation as a comparison	150–152
4.OA.2—Multiply or divide to solve word problems involving multiplicative comparison	153–155
4.OA.3—Solve multistep word problems posed with whole numbers and having whole-number answers	156–158
4.OA.4—Find all factor pairs for a whole number	159–162
4.OA.5—Generate a number or shape pattern that follows a given rule	163–165
Number and Operations in Base Ten	**Page(s)**
4.NBT.1—Recognize that in a multi-digit whole number, a digit in one place represents ten times what it represents in the place to its right.	166–169
4.NBT.2—Read and write multi-digit whole numbers using base-ten numerals, number names, and expanded form	170–173
4.NBT.3—Use place value understanding to round multi-digit whole numbers to any place	174–177
4.NBT.4—Fluently add and subtract multi-digit whole numbers using the standard algorithm	178–184
4.NBT.5—Multiply a whole number up to four digits by a one-digit whole number, and multiply two-digit numbers, using strategies based on place value and the properties of operations	185–191
4.NBT.6—Find whole-number quotients and remainders with up to four-digit dividends and one-digit divisors, using strategies based on place value, the properties of operations, and/or the relationship between multiplication and division	192–196
Number and Operations—Fractions	**Page(s)**
4.NF.1—Explain why a fraction a/b is equivalent to a fraction $(n \times a)/(n \times b)$ by using visual fraction models	197–199
4.NF.2—Compare two fractions with different numerators and different denominators	200–201
4.NF.3—Understand addition and subtraction of fractions as joining and separating parts	202–204
4.NF.3—Decompose a fraction into a sum of fractions with the same denominator in more than one way	205
4.NF.3—Add and subtract mixed numbers with like denominators	206–209
4.NF.3—Solve word problems involving addition and subtraction of fractions	210, 213
4.NF.4—Understand a fraction a/b as a multiple of $1/b$	211–212, 214–215
4.NF.4—Solve word problems involving multiplication of a fraction by a whole number	216–218
4.NF.5—Express a fraction with denominator 10 as an equivalent fraction with denominator 100	219–220
4.NF.6—Use decimal notation for fractions with denominators 10 or 100	221
4.NF.7—Compare two decimals to hundredths by reasoning about their size	222–223
Measurement and Data	**Page(s)**
4.MD.1—Know relative sizes of measurement units with one system of units	224–227
4.MD.2—Use four operations to solve word problems	228–229
4.MD.3—Apply the area and perimeter for rectangles in real world and mathematical problems	230–233
4.MD.4—Make a line plot to display a data set of measurements in fractions of a unit	234–235
4.MD.5—Recognize angles as geometric shapes that are formed wherever two rays share a common endpoint	236–237
4.MD.6—Measure angles in whole-number degrees using a protractor	238–239
4.MD.7—Recognize angle measure as additive	240
Geometry	**Page(s)**
4.G.1—Draw points, lines, segments, rays, angles, and perpendicular and parallel lines	241–243
4.G.2—Classify two-dimensional figures based on the presence or absence of parallel or perpendicular lines	244–246
4.G.3—Recognize a line of symmetry for a two-dimensional figure as a line across the figure such that the figure can be folded along the line into matching parts	247–248

Name: _____ Date: _____

Breaking Up Words

A **syllable** is a single part of a word's pronunciation. Spoken words can be broken down into syllables. Each syllable will always have one vowel sound.

Directions: Circle the correct division of the syllables for each group.

1	eng-ine	engin-e	en-gine
2	weath-er	weat-her	wea-ther
3	ca-stle	cas-tle	cast-le
4	qu-ickly	quic-kly	quick-ly
5	cree-ping	creep-ing	cre-eping
6	foo-tball	footba-ll	foot-ball
7	a-round	arou-nd	aro-und
8	su-nset	suns-et	sun-set
9	doo-rbell	doorb-ell	door-bell
10	extr-a	ext-ra	ex-tra
11	tic-ket	tick-et	ti-cket
12	benea-th	ben-eath	be-neath

Name: _____ Date: _____

Word Division

Directions: Read the list of words aloud. For each word, draw a line to divide the syllables.

1 achieve _____ a / chieve _____

2 product _____

3 capital _____

4 season _____

5 factory _____

6 wetland _____

7 explore _____

8 gender _____

9 city _____

10 economy _____

Name:_____ Date: _____

More Word Division

Directions: Identify the syllables in each word to help you pronounce the word. Place a check mark next to the words that you still need to practice.

_____ admire	_____ entertain
_____ arena	_____ envy
_____ attractive	_____ focus
_____ basic	_____ frequent
_____ capable	_____ hardship
_____ circular	_____ manufacture
_____ concern	_____ peculiar
_____ confuse	_____ prepare
_____ demonstrate	_____ recognize
_____ distract	_____ represent

Directions: Think about how you did reading these words. Then, answer the questions.

❶ How did you use syllables to help you read the words?

_____

_____

_____

_____

❷ What other strategies did you use to read the words?

_____

_____

_____

_____

Name:_____ Date: _____

Decoding Strategies for New Words

Directions: Read the passage. Then, reread the passage following the directions at the bottom of the page.

Constellations

People have been using stars to guide their way and lives for centuries. Without visible landmarks out at sea, mariners depended on compasses and stars to direct their ships. Since the stars served such an important role for people, they named groups of stars to help chart the night sky. We call these star groupings *constellations*.

The constellations have been known by many different names by different groups of people. For example, the ancient Greeks know the Big Dipper as the Bear.

Many of the constellation names were based on ancient stories and myths. Greek mythology claimed that Cassiopeia was more beautiful than the lovely sea nymphs. The nymphs became angry and complained to Poseidon, the god of the sea. Poseidon decided to punish Cassiopeia for her vanity and he sent a sea monster to destroy her kingdom. He then demanded that Cassiopeia's daughter be sacrificed to the sea monster. Fortunately, the young girl was rescued by Perseus before the sea monster could kill her. Cassiopeia was changed into a constellation at her death. She was placed in the night sky for all to remember her.

---

❶ Which words did you decode by breaking them into smaller syllables? Circle those words.

❷ Which words did you reread in order to understand them? Underline those words.

❸ Which words did you have to ask somebody for help to understand? Put a box around those words.

Name: _____ Date: _____

It's All Relative: Using Relative Pronouns

A **pronoun** is a word that replaces a noun, such as *he*, *me*, or *we*.

A **relative pronoun** introduces a **relative clause**.

There are five relative pronouns: *that*, *which*, *who*, *whom*, and *whose*.

Directions: Complete the following sentences with the correct relative pronoun.

1 The letter _____ you gave me was very thoughtful and kind.

2 Babe Ruth, _____ is still one of the greatest athletes in all of American sports, will never be forgotten.

3 A fourth grader, _____ main job is to work hard in school, is still learning how to be responsible.

4 Ramona ordered the chocolate cake, _____ is why her sister made the same choice.

5 The library's children's section was full of students, almost all of _____ were looking for research books for their reports that are due on Friday.

6 My favorite pizza topping is pepperoni, _____ was the most popular response in the class survey.

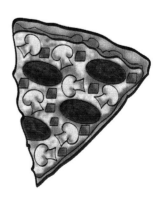

Name: _____ Date: _____

Writing with Relative Pronouns

Directions: Write a sentence for each relative pronoun to show the correct way to use it in a sentence.

1 *that*

_____

_____

2 *which*

_____

_____

3 *who*

_____

_____

4 *whom*

_____

_____

5 *whose*

_____

_____

Directions: Write a short paragraph that includes more than one relative pronoun.

_____

_____

_____

_____

_____

_____

_____

_____

Name:_____ Date: _____

Finding Relative Pronouns in Literature

Directions: Go on a search for relative pronouns in the stories and textbooks that you are reading. Record your examples in the chart below.

Relative pronoun example	Where you found it	Who wrote it

What did you learn about relative pronouns by studying these examples?

_____

_____

_____

_____

_____

Name:_____ Date: _____

Adverbs Tell Us More About the Action

Adverbs are describing words that tell more about a verb. They tell *when* (a time), *where* (a place), or *how* (how something is done).

A **relative adverb** joins clauses. Relative adverbs include *when*, *where*, and *why*.

Directions: Complete the sentences with the correct relative adverb.

1 Do you know the reason _____ our theater coach said that I would not be the best lead in the fourth grade play?

2 Ferndale Park is the place _____ our end-of-the-summer picnic will be held in August.

3 November is _____ I can make a lot of extra cash by raking up the fall leaves for neighbors.

4 Six o'clock is _____ we normally eat dinner, but tonight we are eating early so that we can go see the movie in the park.

5 A parking ticket is the reason _____ my mom has to go to city hall to pay a fine.

6 Second grade was a great year, _____ I met my best friend, and _____ I discovered that I loved math more than any other subject.

7 Since I just started school here yesterday, my classmates reminded me that the blue shelf is _____ we put away our journals.

8 My grandmother says that the reason _____ her family came to America was to have a better life.

Name:_____ Date: _____

Making Relative Adverbs Personal

Directions: Using the topics provided, write sentences for each relative adverb to show the correct way to use it into a sentence.

1 **relative adverb:** when   **topic:** your favorite holiday

_____

_____

_____

2 **relative adverb:** when   **topic:** something you enjoy doing during recess

_____

_____

_____

3 **relative adverb:** when   **topic:** your typical morning

_____

_____

_____

4 **relative adverb:** where   **topic:** your favorite vacation

_____

_____

_____

5 **relative adverb:** where   **topic:** a place you have always wanted to visit

_____

_____

_____

6 **relative adverb:** why   **topic:** where you eat lunch everyday

_____

_____

_____

Name:_____ Date: _____

Alternatives to Using Relative Adverbs?

Some relative adverbs are optional and can be left out of sentences if the sentences are still grammatically correct.

Example:
My friend says the reason <u>that</u> she is late every day is because her alarm clock is broken.

Directions: Go on a search for relative adverbs in the stories and textbooks that you are reading. Record your examples in the chart below.

Relative Adverb Example	Where you Found It	Who Wrote It

Write an example of a sentence that you found that can be rewritten without its relative adverb.

_____

_____

_____

_____

_____

_____

Name:_____ Date: _____

Progressive Verbs

Directions: Read the following sentences. Decide which progressive form of the verb needs to be included in the spaces.

1 Hector _____ in a soccer game later today, but right now he is resting. (*play*)

2 The monkey _____ up the tree when we were watching him at the zoo. (*climb*)

3 If you _____ past breakfast, then you will miss eggs and bacon! (*sleep*)

4 I stop by Room 2 and notice that the teacher _____ her class a warning for talking too much during work time. (*give*)

5 My mother told me this morning that I _____ my thank you notes today until they are completed. (*write*)

6 Our dog _____ his dinner when he heard something scary and jumped up and howled. (*eat*)

7 Maria _____ in next Saturday's race in honor of her mom who died earlier in the year. (*run*)

8 When the music stops, I will ask who _____ on a certain number to win the game. (*stand*)

Name:_____ Date: _____

Showing Progression Through Pictures

The **progressive forms** of a verb show how a verb tense changes depending on when the action takes place.

Directions: Write an example to show how these forms of progressive verbs are different.

is/am/are giving	was/were giving	will be giving

is/am/are watching	was/were watching	will be watching

Name:_____ Date: _____

Verbs: Writing Progressive Forms

The **progressive forms** of a verb show how a verb tense changes depending on when the action takes place.

Directions: Look at the verbs below. Write two sentences using different progressive forms of each verb.

see

❶ _____

_____

❷ _____

_____

laugh

❶ _____

_____

❷ _____

_____

run

❶ _____

_____

❷ _____

_____

read

❶ _____

_____

❷ _____

_____

Name: _____ Date: _____

Getting into Modal Auxiliary Verbs

A **modal auxiliary verb** is a verb that is used to indicate *modality*, which is a scale ranging from a possibility (*may*) to a necessity (*must*). They are called "helping verbs" because they help tell more about the main verb that follows.

Directions: Based on your own experiences, complete the sentences below using the modal auxiliary verbs provided.

1 I can _____ .

2 I could _____ .

3 I may _____ .

4 I might _____ .

5 I must _____ .

6 I ought to _____ .

7 I shall _____ .

8 I should _____ .

9 I will _____ .

10 I would _____ .

Directions: Based on another individual's experiences, complete the sentences below using the modal auxiliary verbs provided.

1 _____ can _____ .

2 _____ could _____ .

Name: _____ Date: _____

Adding the Auxiliaries

Directions: Complete each of the following sentences with a modal auxiliary verb that makes sense. There may be more than one correct answer for each sentence.

Word Bank

can	could	may	might
must	ought to	shall	would

---

1 The football players _____ get good grades in order to play in Friday's game.

2 My sister _____ cry louder than any other four-year-old I have ever known.

3 Owen's mom _____ pick me up if she has time in the morning, or else I can ride the bus.

4 I know that I _____ take out the garbage to help out my dad, but I really want to finish this video game.

5 After years of swim lessons, I _____ finally do the backstroke for the whole length of the pool!

6 Tomorrow _____ be the first time that I get to eat popcorn since my braces came off.

7 My teacher says that wearing sandals to school _____ be a problem if I fall during recess.

8 The parade _____ go down Main Street because I see the signs saying the road is closed.

Name:_____ Date: _____

Putting Adjectives in Order

Adjectives are words that describe people, places, and things.

When a sentence has more than one adjective, this is how the adjectives should be listed:

- Determiners come first.
  Articles (*a*, *the*), possessives (*my*, *your*), demonstratives (*this*, *that*), quantifiers (*some*, *any*, *few*, *many*), and numbers (*one*, *two*, *three*) are all determiners.

- Opinions come next.

- Fact adjectives come next.
  The normal order for fact adjectives is size, age, color, material, and shape.

Directions: Rewrite the sentences with the adjectives in the correct order.

1 There was a black, small, disgusting spider hanging from the web in the corner of the room.

_____

_____

2 The old, sweet, tall man came to the door and asked what we wanted.

_____

_____

3 Those leather, black, fancy shoes are way too small for me now.

_____

_____

4 The yellow, small, gorgeous, daffodil flowers are in a vase on my table.

_____

_____

5 The night was quiet when the brown, large, spooky barn owl began to hoot.

_____

_____

Name: _____ Date: _____

Writing Sequenced Adjectives

Directions: Write a sentence for each group of adjectives in the correct order.

1 red, large, wooden

_____

_____

_____

2 orange, small, beautiful

_____

_____

_____

3 purple, old, delicate

_____

_____

_____

4 blue, tiny, square

_____

_____

_____

5 black, glass, round, enormous

_____

_____

_____

6 yellow, organic, vegetable

_____

_____

_____

Name:_____ Date: _____

Adjectives Complete the Story

Directions: Add adjectives to complete the story.

A Nice Surprise

It was my _____ birthday, so I ran home from school.
When I got to my _____ house, it looked like no one
was home. "Where is my _____ family?" I wondered.
I went to our _____ kitchen to see if there was a note.
No note. Not even a _____ note. I went into the
_____ room and turned on the _____
television. I couldn't find a _____ show to watch. "I
want something that is _____ to eat," I said to myself. I
found _____ yogurt and _____ bread. I
was just about to eat it when the _____ telephone rang.

It was my mom. "Honey," my mom said. "Please come to our neighbor's
_____ house next door." "Why?" I asked. "Because I
need you to help me carry something home."

That made me wonder. "Did she have a _____ present
for me? Was it so _____ that she couldn't even carry it
herself?"

As I walked to the _____ house, I started to think that I
had it all wrong. I knew we were meeting my dad later for dinner at the
_____ restaurant. That's when we would celebrate.

I knocked on the _____ door. I didn't hear anything.
"Did my mom leave?" I was getting irritated. Finally she opened the
_____ door. I walked into my neighbor's house. Just
then, I heard _____ voices shouting, "Happy Birthday!"
My heart was pounding so hard I thought it would beat out of my
_____ chest! I saw a house full of _____
people. They were holding _____ balloons and
_____ gifts.

Name:_____ Date: _____

It's Just a Phrase: Prepositional Phrases

A **preposition** is a word or group of words that combine with nouns or pronouns to show direction, location, time, or to introduce an object.

A **prepositional phrase** includes a preposition and other words to help clarify this relationship. It gives more information and elaborates on a subject.

Directions: Write a sentence using a prepositional phrase that describes the relationship of the subjects in the pictures.

❶

_____
_____
_____

❷

_____
_____
_____

❸

_____
_____
_____

❹

_____
_____
_____

Name: _____ Date: _____

Writing Prepositional Phrases

Directions: Write a sentence using a prepositional phrase that describes the relationship between each pair of items listed below.

1 a bell and a cow

_____

_____

2 a rattle and a baby

_____

_____

3 an airplane and a runway

_____

_____

4 a foot and a shoe

_____

_____

5 a flag and a building

_____

_____

6 a scoop of ice cream and a cone

_____

_____

7 a barn and a farmer

_____

_____

8 a scarf and a snowman

_____

_____

Name: _____ Date: _____

More on the Preposition

· ·

Directions: Write a sentence using the prepositions listed below.

1 underneath

_____

_____

2 between

_____

_____

3 against

_____

_____

4 within

_____

_____

5 throughout

_____

_____

6 past

_____

_____

7 upon

_____

_____

8 after

_____

_____

Name: _____ Date: _____

Complete That Sentence!

> A **sentence** is a group of words that tells us something or asks us a question. It is always a complete thought.

Directions: If it is a complete sentence, write the letter C. If it is an incomplete sentence, write the letter I.

❶ _____ Over the rainbow!

❷ _____ Becky writes a letter.

❸ _____ Does Jamie want?

❹ _____ Strawberries and bananas.

❺ _____ Watch out for the ball!

❻ _____ When school over?

❼ _____ I am in the pool.

❽ _____ When Derek

❾ _____ Do you like dogs?

❿ _____ I can see you!

Directions: Now, write three complete sentences of your own. Remember to end with the correct punctuation mark.

_____

_____

_____

_____

_____

_____

Name:_____ Date: _____

Stop That Run-On Sentence

Some sentences do not stop when they should. A sentence that runs on to the next thought is called a **run-on sentence.**

Directions: Each of the following sentences is a run-on sentence. Write each run-on sentence as two separate sentences.

1 My books are on the table my math book is on top.

_____

_____

_____

2 They were closing the store it was time to go home.

_____

_____

_____

3 Watch out for the slippery ice you could fall and hurt yourself.

_____

_____

_____

4 I got a new blue dress the blue shoes match perfectly.

_____

_____

_____

5 My brother made the team will I be able to play baseball some day?

_____

_____

_____

Name:_____ Date: _____

Piecing Together Sentence Fragments

A **sentence fragment** is a sentence that has an incomplete thought. A sentence fragment is usually missing a piece of information.

Directions: Use your imagination to rewrite the fragments below as complete sentences with capital letters and ending punctuation.

1 went flying in the air _____

_____

2 my best friend _____

_____

3 Manny's birthday party _____

_____

4 fell off the fence _____

_____

5 was blowing big bubbles _____

_____

6 a giant spider _____

_____

7 ran into the street _____

_____

8 her hamster _____

_____

Name:_____ Date: _____

Essential Homophones: They're, You're, and It's

Some words sound the same but they are spelled differently and mean different things. These words are called **homophones**.

Directions: Circle the correct homophones in the sentences below.

1 (Its, It's) wonderful that the circus will be here on Saturday.

2 (Your, You're) lucky to have tickets.

3 (Their, They're, There) is always a lot of excitement when the lights first go off.

4 The trainers will walk out with (their, they're, there) animals in the opening parade.

5 The elephant will walk with a trainer on (its, it's) back.

6 Don't leave (your, you're) seats until intermission, so you don't miss anything!

7 The acrobats are always nervous because (there, their, they're) doing a dangerous and risky act on the high wire.

8 (Its, It's) the best show in town tonight so make sure you have (your, you're) ticket!

Name: _____ Date: _____

To, Too, or Two?

Directions: Write the correct meaning of to, too, or two on the lines below.

1 I'm going _____ be in a dance recital tomorrow. I'll be wearing my new tutu, which is a little _____ big. _____ of my friends will dance, _____.

I'm _____ excited _____ sleep, but I have _____ go _____ bed.

2 The leaves were falling from the trees as I walked _____ school. It must be fall, which I call autumn, _____. I know that there are _____ more weeks until Halloween. I can't wait _____ go trick or treating! My friend Alexa is going _____ walk with me, _____. We will remember _____ say "Thank You!" after we get our candy. I hope that I get at least _____ lollipops to eat!

Name:_____ Date: _____

Spell It Out Correctly

Directions: Write a sentence that models the correct usage for each homophone.

their	they're	there
_____	_____	_____
_____	_____	_____
_____	_____	_____
_____	_____	_____
_____	_____	_____

its	it's
_____	_____
_____	_____
_____	_____

your	you're
_____	_____
_____	_____
_____	_____

Name:_____ Date: _____

Capital with a *C*

Directions: Circle the letters that needs to be capitalized.

1 when i went to the store, i saw mrs. cooper buying strawberries.

2 my family will go to disneyland in july.

3 i am reading *old yeller* this week.

4 my sister, sarah, says her favorite holiday is halloween.

5 on thursday, we will celebrate thanksgiving.

6 our neighbor is a cheerleader at roosevelt high school.

7 in august, we are going to visit aunt margaret in san francisco, california.

8 my friend, rosa, went to springfield and i went to new york city.

9 my little brother had to see dr. may for an ear infection.

10 dad was not happy that i was late getting home.

Name:_____ Date: _____

Specials Titles Deserve Special Letters

Titles of books, movies, plays, magazines, newspapers, or works of art are all capitalized. The rule is to capitalize the first word, the last word, and every word in between except for *a, an, the, short prepositions (in, on)*, and *short conjunctions (and, but)*.

Directions: Answer each of the following questions. Write a complete sentence.

1 What is your favorite book? _____

_____

_____

_____

2 Who is your favorite author? _____

_____

_____

_____

3 What newspaper is delivered in your town? _____

_____

_____

_____

4 What is the name of the last movie that you watched? _____

_____

_____

_____

5 What movie could you watch every single day? _____

_____

_____

_____

Name:_____ Date: _____

Answering with Capitals

Directions: Answer the questions below. Write a complete sentence.

1 What is your full name? _____

_____

_____

_____

2 What is your favorite place to visit? _____

_____

_____

_____

3 Which holiday tradition do you enjoy the most? _____

_____

_____

_____

4 What is your favorite day of the week? Why? _____

_____

_____

_____

5 When do you celebrate your birthday? _____

_____

_____

_____

6 Where did you go on your last vacation? _____

_____

_____

_____

Name: _____ Date: _____

"What's That You Say?"

Quotation marks are placed around a person's exact words when speaking. This is called a direct quotation. Commas are used to separate the quote from the rest of the sentence.

Directions: Add quotation marks and commas in the correct places.

1 Why is the principal coming in our room Mrs. Carter's students wondered.

2 Hector teased You are going to be in last place.

3 Please hang up your backpacks Mr. Fox called out before you sit at your desk.

4 Where is the ice cream social being held tonight my mom asked me after school.

5 Jason shouted I am not happy about my soccer team's loss!

6 I don't think I can come to your party Fiona told me because I have a family gathering to go to.

7 What animals would you expect to see in the Amazon rain forest Mrs. Garcia asked.

8 The teacher commented When we study space you will learn about comets and meteors.

Name:_____ Date: _____

Quoting and Punctuating

A **direct quotation** always begins with a capital letter no matter where the quotation appears in the sentence. However, the end punctuation in the quotation varies depending on the placement.

Speaker Before: A comma comes before the quote. The quote has punctuation like a regular sentence and is enclosed by quotation marks.	*Speaker Between:* A comma comes before the quote. Then, the speaker is identified, followed by another comma before the quote continues.	*Speaker After:* If the quote is a question or exclamation, it has the correct ending punctuation. If the quote is a sentence, a comma is used instead of a period.

Directions: Rewrite the following sentences, adding punctuation marks, quotation marks, and capitalization as needed.

1 Michael shouted let's get busy with the paint

_____

_____

_____

2 Has anyone in this group ever climbed Mount Everest asked the mountain guide

_____

_____

_____

3 Mr. Cumming said please watch your step through the pond

_____

_____

_____

Name: _____ Date: _____

Conjunction Commas

> A **coordinating conjunction** connects three or more items in a series. They connect words, phrases, and clauses. There are seven coordinating conjunctions: and, but, for, nor, or, so, and yet.
>
> Use a comma when you connect two main clauses.
>
> *Example:* He liked the movie, but it was not his favorite.

Directions: Rewrite the following sentences using a coordinating conjunction and a comma to connect them.

1 We went to a great concert last night. The music was too loud.

_____

_____

_____

2 George likes to play soccer during recess. His friend Adam likes to play baseball.

_____

_____

_____

3 The fire raged on all through the night. The firemen felt exhausted by the break of the day.

_____

_____

_____

4 Raymond had trouble sleeping that night. The next day was his birthday.

_____

_____

_____

Name: _____ Date: _____

Adding Commas to the List

> A **coordinating conjunction** can be used to connect words in a series. Three or more items together make a series.
>
> *Example:* We will be talking today about planets, meteors, and comets.

Directions: Add the missing commas to the sentences below.

1 All birds have feathers wings and beaks.

2 My sister is hungry sleepy and grumpy.

3 I ordered a pizza with pepperoni mushrooms and olives.

4 This rule applies to Jake Cindia and yourself.

5 Lily would have finished her homework but she had a late soccer practice and fell asleep early.

6 My dog has brown spots a short tail and fuzzy feet.

7 The birthday party was planned for the park but it was rainy that day and my mom decided that indoors was better.

8 Can you go to the store and get butter flour and milk?

9 When I go on vacation, I am taking a suitcase my bike and a camera.

10 Did your friend want a book clothes or a DVD for her birthday?

Name:_____ Date: _____

Dictionary Definitions

Directions: Look up these words in a dictionary. Write the definition in your own words and a short sentence that correctly uses the word.

❶ *sinister*

Definition: _____

_____

_____

_____

_____

Sentence: _____

_____

_____

_____

_____

❷ *plague*

Definition: _____

_____

_____

_____

_____

Sentence: _____

_____

_____

_____

_____

❸ *distraught*

Definition: _____

_____

_____

_____

Sentence: _____

_____

_____

_____

_____

❹ *atmosphere*

Definition: _____

_____

_____

_____

Sentence: _____

_____

_____

_____

_____

Name:_____ Date: _____

A Friendly Dictionary

. . . .

Directions: Fill out the chart below with words you are looking for in a dictionary. Use guide words to help you find the words more easily.

Unfamiliar Word	Part of Speech (noun, verb, adjective?)	Definition (in your own words)

Name: _____ Date: _____

Show Me, Don't Tell Me

Many writers try to include specific words to describe actions and appearances. They want to *show* readers something, rather than *tell* them.

Telling the reader: Julie is a bully.

Showing the reader: Julie intentionally stuck out her leg as Timmy walked by. As Timmy tripped, Julie laughed in his face. "Gotcha again, Timmy boy!" she jeered.

Directions: Read the sentences and change them from telling sentences to showing sentences.

1 The puppy is cute. _____

_____

_____

_____

2 My teacher is so nice. _____

_____

_____

_____

3 The house looked abandoned. _____

_____

_____

_____

4 My little brother is helpful. _____

_____

_____

_____

Name:_____ Date: _____

Vivid Verbs: Using Descriptive Words

Directions: Rewrite the sentences using more vivid verbs and descriptive language.

1 The audience *called loudly* for an encore.

_____

_____

_____

_____

2 The dog *went* around the block with his owner.

_____

_____

_____

_____

3 Simon *said* he wanted an ice cream cone right now.

_____

_____

_____

_____

4 The two girls *walked* to the swimming pool on the hot day.

_____

_____

_____

_____

Name:_____ Date: _____

Description Riddles

Directions: Read the three riddles below. Read the language carefully and think about how the words help you understand what they are trying to describe.

Riddle #1

I am a great ball of fire. I paint a new picture on my canvas before retiring each night. Sometimes I fight the clouds with my paintbrushes, and they let me have some space. When I turn off my light, people turn on theirs.

What am I? _____

Riddle #2

I carry people to their destinations, for I never tire. People push my buttons all day, but I don't get upset. Sometimes, an "out of order" sign is placed on me, and boy, do some people get angry! My doors open and close, open and close, and I never become confused about where I am or what floor I'm on. I guess you could say I'm pretty smart. The stairs get jealous, but hey, that's just too bad.

What am I? _____

Riddle #3

I really don't mind getting kicked around. I like the colors black and white. Sometimes I get wet, other times I get muddy. But, that doesn't bother me at all. I like the sounds of the kids laughing as they play with me. And, the best part of my day is when I get to go inside the net. People always cheer when they see me go in there!

What am I? _____

Name: _____ Date: _____

The Order in the Phrase

> Writers like to change the structure of their sentences so that their writing does not begin to sound dull to readers.
>
> *Example:* The lost child glanced up each aisle in the busy grocery store, looking for her mother.
>
> *Revision:* Glancing up each aisle, the lost child looked for her mother in the busy grocery store.

Directions: Think about how the words are ordered. Revise each sentence.

1 The red balloon floated into the cloud-filled sky.

Revision: _____

_____

_____

2 As people watched, a crane came to the building and knocked it down with a wrecking ball.

Revision: _____

_____

_____

3 Swinging his axe, the woodsman chopped down a tree to use for his log cabin.

Revision: _____

_____

_____

4 In the cool shade, the two kids rested in a hammock and ate ice cream cones.

Revision: _____

_____

_____

Name:_____ Date: _____

Powerful Ending Punctuation

> **Declarative sentences** are "telling" sentences that end with a period.
>
> **Interrogative sentences** are sentences that ask questions and end with a question mark.
>
> **Exclamatory sentences** show strong feelings, emotions, or surprise and end with an exclamation mark.

Directions: Add ending punctuation to the sentences. Then, identify if the sentence is a declarative sentence, interrogative sentence, or an exclamatory sentence.

1 What happened to the girl who broke her leg during the soccer game

_____

2 The team was so worried about her after watching her cry

_____

3 Please be careful, everyone

_____

4 The team gathered to have a snack after the game and greet their opponents

_____

5 How did the other team feel that one of our players got hurt

_____

6 Our coaches talked with us about what it means to show good sportsmanship.

_____

Name: _____ Date: _____

Emphasizing Information with Commas

Commas are included in writing to tell readers when to slow down, but their placement can be used strategically to emphasize certain information. Commas often set off phrases and clauses.

Directions: Add missing commas to set off phrases and emphasize certain information.

1 The blue whale measuring 98 feet in length is the largest known animal to have ever existed.

2 The carnival ride The Spinning Top can make people sick when it starts moving fast.

3 We went to Richardson Park a wonderful open space near downtown to celebrate my birthday.

4 For Valentine's Day my dad gave me my favorite treat.

5 My brother the world's most annoying six-year-old would not stop bothering me this morning.

6 The United States of America our great nation will celebrate its birthday on the Fourth of July.

7 The Amazon Rainforest the most magnificent place in the world is home to thousands of interesting plant and animal species.

8 The plane we are taking a 747 will have plenty of room.

9 The day after my party Kevin called to apologize for missing out on the fun.

10 The referee after consulting with other officials on the field called a penalty on the player.

Name:_____ Date: _____

Parenthetical Expressions

Commas can be included in sentences as side remarks that interrupt the main ideas of sentences. These interrupting remarks are called **parenthetical expressions**.

Commonly Used Parenthetical Expressions:

- after all
- at any rate
- by the way
- I suppose

- in my opinion
- on the other hand
- I believe
- I think

- however
- therefore
- nevertheless
- of course

- on the contrary
- for instance
- to say the least
- for example

Directions: Write a word or phrase that makes sense and add commas where they are needed. *Note:* There is more than one correct answer.

❶ This package is addressed to you _____ and needs to be opened.

❷ The president _____ said he hopes to do better next term.

❸ _____ I hope you learn to swim this summer.

❹ Many animals _____ are slowly becoming extinct.

❺ Do you know _____ when the next train will arrive?

❻ I want to invite Tate _____ to my party on Saturday.

Directions: Write a sentence using parenthetical expressions.

_____

_____

_____

Name: _____ Date: _____

Punctuating a Paragraph

Directions: Add the correct punctuation to the paragraphs below.

Dear Grandma

Thank you so much for sending me the wonderful birthday present How did you know that I needed a green sweater It even came from my favorite store I had a wonderful day My friend Lily helped my parents throw me a surprise party Of course I had no idea I was so shocked to say the least My parents and my friends made me feel like the luckiest girl

I hope I get to see you soon It's been too long I think

Love

Katy

Name:_____ Date: _____

Formal vs. Informal:
When to Choose a Writing Style

Directions: Read the paragraph. Then, write about why the particular style does not seem appropriate for the material.

Spring

Learning about the seasons is way cool! Spring is, like, the best part of the year. Wow! It blows my mind how many things come alive at that time of year. Plants are for sure blooming. They are pushing up through the ground and trying to bloom. It's so cute!

The awesome, warm sun helps melt the snow on the mountains. Then, the rivers and streams are crazy full of water! They help bring water to places that are dry. New animals and plants need this water because they are thirsty.

I can't wait to investigate all that has changed in the nearby woods since the snow started to melt. My parents will flip out, too! Nature is pretty amazing.

❶ How would you describe the style of this story?

_____
_____
_____

❷ Why does this style not match the content of the story?

_____
_____
_____

❸ What kind of writing could use this style?

_____
_____
_____

Name:_____ Date: _____

Practicing Informal and Formal Writing

Directions: Pick two topics to write paragraphs about. Write one paragraph in an informal style, and then write the other topic in a formal style.

Informal Writing
Topic: _____
_____
_____
_____
_____
_____
_____
_____
_____

Formal Writing
Topic: _____
_____
_____
_____
_____
_____
_____
_____
_____

Name:_____ Date: _____

Making Inferences in Daily Life

Directions: Practice making inferences by drawing conclusions based on the short, real-world scenarios below.

1 The bus station is full of people, perhaps three times as many as normal. Passengers look frustrated and annoyed. It is the first rainy morning of the year and the radio news is sharing that there are several car accidents all over town.

What might be happening? _____

_____

_____

_____

_____

_____

2 The park ranger lights a match and smiles. He adds extra wood to the fire. It is autumn now, and the national park is fairly quiet. This is a perfect way to end the season.

What might be happening? _____

_____

_____

_____

_____

_____

3 The lights on the street go dark. It happens all at once, like someone just flipped a switch. Televisions, computers, telephones—they all don't work right now. There is not much to do but light a candle and wait.

What might be happening? _____

_____

_____

_____

_____

_____

Name:_____ Date: _____

Explicit Details and Implicit Inferences

Directions: Pick an informational text to read. As you read, look for details and examples that are directly stated (explicit), as well as ones that force you to draw inferences (implicit). Then, fill out the chart below.

Implicit				
Explicit				
Details and Examples				
Title and Author				

Name: _____ Date: _____

The Big Idea

Every paragraph in an informational text has sentences in a special order. The sentences work together to develop a **main idea**, or the big idea of the paragraph.

Directions: Cross out the idea in each list that does not relate to the main idea.

❶ inside my house bathroom living room attic bedroom football field kitchen	**❻ animals** cat dog predator zoo sky tiger
❷ food beans towels corn spinach bread tomatoes	**❼ homework** eraser ruler calculator pencil crayons television
❸ colors blue lavender beige black magenta hairy	**❽ musical instruments** piano violin drums cello shoe harmonica
❹ sports soccer lacrosse leaf helmet referee net	**❾ tools** hammer nail tool belt screw saw diving board
❺ countries New York Ireland Brazil Costa Rica France USA	**❿ clothes** jacket button socks pizza denim zipper

Name:_____ Date: _____

A Paragraph's Main Idea

A **main idea** is the big idea of a paragraph or story. It is the main point that the author is trying to make to the reader. The author then uses **supporting details** to prove the main idea of the text.

Directions: Decide what the main idea is. Write about the supporting details as well.

The animal kingdom is divided into two groups. One group is the invertebrates, creatures without backbones. The second group is the vertebrates, those with backbones. All mammals, such as dogs and human beings, have backbones. A backbone is a row of small bone blocks running down a mammal's back. It is strong, and it protects the spinal cord, which is like a rope of nerves. The backbone also bends and twists.

❶ What is the main idea of the paragraph?

_____

_____

_____

_____

_____

_____

❷ What are some of the supporting details in the paragraph?

_____

_____

_____

_____

_____

_____

_____

_____

Name:_____ Date: _____

What's It All About?

A **main idea** is the big idea of a paragraph or story. It is the main point that the author is trying to make to the reader. The author then uses **supporting details** to prove the main idea of the text.

Directions: Read the informational text. Then, answer the questions.

Fossils give clues about what happened in Earth's history. To tell how old rocks are, scientists study the fossils in them. Fossils are mainly found in rock that used to be mud millions of years ago. Most fossils are of animals with shells and tiny parts of plants and animals. Some fossils are so small they must be studied under a microscope. These are the kind scientists study the most.

Does the word *fossil* make you think of dinosaurs? Dinosaurs appear in books, movies, and television programs. The bones of some large dinosaurs are in many museums. These reptiles lived on Earth for well over 100 million years. By around 65 million years ago, all dinosaurs were extinct. Why they disappeared and what made them disappear so quickly are unanswered.

Paleontologists are the scientists that are most interested in fossils. They are trying to uncover new clues about dinosaur species. Archaeologists tend to be more interested in artifacts. These are the remains of things that were made by humans. Fossils, on the other hand, are the remains of living things.

❶ What is the main idea of the text?

_____

_____

❷ List some of the supporting details in the text.

_____

_____

_____

Name:_____ Date: _____

Identifying Main Idea Graphic Organizer

Directions: Use the graphic organizer to record the main idea and supporting details in a piece of informational text you are reading.

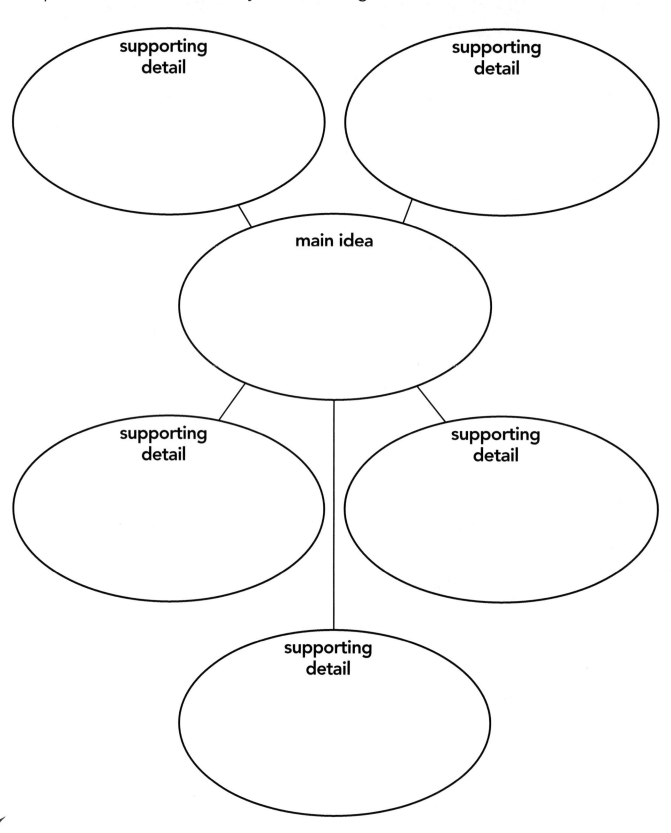

#50908—*Bright & Brainy: 4th Grade Practice* © *Shell Education*

Name:_____ Date: _____

Summarizing Life Experiences

Directions: Answer these questions about your own life by only sharing the most important details.

1 Describe what you did last weekend.

_____

_____

_____

_____

_____

_____

_____

2 Describe your favorite birthday celebration.

_____

_____

_____

_____

_____

_____

_____

3 Write about your favorite thing about school.

_____

_____

_____

_____

_____

_____

_____

Name:_____ Date: _____

Explaining by Summarizing

. . . .

Summarizing is retelling the most important ideas of what a text is about.

Directions: Read the paragraph and write a short paragraph summarizing what you have read. Include the main idea and the most important details.

Butterflies are beautiful insects. They flitter around in the spring air. They rest upon the tulips and daisies.

Butterflies can be dark brown, bright yellow, orange, blue, or any number of colors. They begin life as caterpillars. Then, they spin silky covers called cocoons. Inside the cocoon, the caterpillar turns into a butterfly. Butterflies help to spread pollen from one flower to another, so butterflies are helpful as well as beautiful.

Summarize the paragraph above.

_____

_____

_____

_____

_____

_____

_____

_____

_____

_____

_____

_____

Name:_____ Date: _____

Summarizing Informational Texts

A **summary** is a short statement about a text. It highlights the main points and most important details.

Directions: After reading an informational text, use the questions—Who? What? When? Where? Why? How?—to describe the key facts. Then, use your answers to write a short summary.

Who? _____

_____

What? _____

_____

When? _____

_____

Where? _____

_____

Why? _____

_____

How? _____

_____

Summary: _____

_____

_____

_____

_____

_____

_____

_____

Name: _____ Date: _____

Academic Words in Context

> **Academic words** are words that are commonly used across different subject areas at school. Words like *consequence, identify, perspective,* and *revise* are all examples of academic words.

Directions: Use context clues to determine the meaning of the underlined academic words. Write the definitions on the lines.

1 The <u>sequence</u> of events that led to the Civil War began years before.

_____

_____

2 One <u>factor</u> that caused the birds to die in great numbers was the use of chemicals that weakened the shells of their eggs.

_____

_____

3 Harbor seals will eat a <u>variety</u> of fish. Their diet changes due to seasons and what fish are available.

_____

_____

4 Air pollution can <u>influence</u> the health of all living things. The effects on human health are serious.

_____

_____

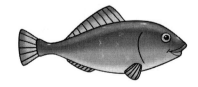

Name:_____ Date: _____

Making Connections to Vocabulary

Directions: Read the informational passage. Then, answer the questions.

The Earth Moves

The ground shakes when the Earth's crust moves. This is called an earthquake. It is caused by the crust sliding, volcanic bursts, or man-made explosions. The crust sliding causes the most *extreme* damage.

At first, the crust may only bend because of pushing forces. When the pushing becomes too much, the crust snaps and shifts into a new position. This causes seismic waves.

Movement of the crust may leave a crack, or fault, in the land. Geologists who *examine* these faults say that earthquakes often happen where there are old faults. These are weak places in the crust. Where there are faults, earthquakes may happen again and again. If these locations are adjacent to a populated area, people living there will likely experience more earthquakes.

It is difficult to *foreshadow* the beginnings of an earthquake. They usually happen suddenly and with little warning. It is usually after the event when people can *reflect* on what happened and how it felt.

---

1 Write about a time that you had to use <u>extreme</u> behavior in order to make something happen.

_____

_____

_____

2 What is an example of how to <u>examine</u> a situation from different perspectives?

_____

_____

_____

Name: _____ Date: _____

Comparing and Contrasting Academic Words

Directions: Read the passage. It has two pairs of vocabulary words to study. Write about how the words are similar and different.

Where Did the Dinosaurs Go?

A common *belief* among many paleontologists is that a giant asteroid or comet can be linked to the extinction of dinosaurs. These scientists *claim* that the change happened very quickly. Clouds of dust blocked the sun, turning the planet into a cold and dark landscape.

Scientists use evidence to clarify their conclusions. The existence of a crater lies just off the Yucatan peninsula. Researchers say that the size of the crater does indicate a large impact. But, there is really no way to know for sure.

Scientists will continue to study fossils, rocks, and other indicators of what life was like many years ago. It is a 65 million-year-old mystery.

---

1 How are the words *belief* and *claim* similar?

_____

_____

_____

_____

2 How are the words *belief* and *claim* different?

_____

_____

_____

_____

Name:_____ Date: _____

Vocabulary Diagram

A **vocabulary diagram** is a graphic organizer that helps you think about a new vocabulary word in different ways.

Directions: Choose an academic vocabulary word from an informational text that you are reading. Fill out the different categories on the vocabulary diagram below.

Synonyms: Antonyms:	Word:	Other forms of the word:
Sentence in text:	Picture:	Original sentence of your own:

Name:_____ Date: _____

Chronological Order in Writing

Some nonfiction texts are written in **chronological** order. This means that the events of the text are written in the order in which they occur.

Directions: Read the following groups of events. Within each group, place the events in chronological order. Mark the first event with a 1 and the last event with a 5.

❶ _____ eat breakfast

_____ get up

_____ go to school

_____ go out the door

_____ brush teeth

❷ _____ afternoon bell rings

_____ lunch recess

_____ morning recess

_____ morning bell rings

_____ after-school care begins

❸ _____ the referee blows the whistle
for the game to begin

_____ girls cheer the other team and
enjoy an after-game snack

_____ halftime

_____ the players greet each other and wish each other a good game

_____ the whistle indicates that the game is over

Name:_____ Date: _____

Determining Text Order

Directions: Read the text. Then, answer the questions.

How to Make Pizza Dough

Making pizza dough is easy and fun to do! First, mix warm water and yeast in a large bowl. Next, add the salt, oil, and flour. Then, knead the dough very carefully by pressing it firmly with your hands against a well-floured surface. Finally, let the yeast do its magic and allow the bread to rise for one hour. When you are all done, your dough is ready to be rolled out. All it needs is tomato sauce, cheese, and toppings….and you are ready to bake your pizza!

1 What do you do first to make pizza dough?

_____

_____

2 What do you do after mixing water and yeast?

_____

_____

3 What is the last step to do with the dough?

_____

_____

4 What key words did the author use that helped you figure out the chronological order of the story?

_____

_____

Name:_____ Date: _____

Mapping a Chronological Text

Directions: Pick a story and summarize the chronological events that occur in the story.

Beginning

↓

Middle

↓

Middle

↓

Middle

↓

End

Name:_____ Date: _____

Comparing and Contrasting Two Topics

Directions: Read the topic pairs. For each pair, write a few similarities and differences between the two.

Topics: baseball and football

Similarities: _____

_____

_____

Differences: _____

_____

_____

Topics: summer and winter

Similarities: _____

_____

_____

Differences: _____

_____

_____

Topics: math and science

Similarities: _____

_____

_____

Differences: _____

_____

_____

Name:_____ Date: _____

Tale of Two Documents

Directions: Read the passage below. Then, answer the questions.

Two Documents in History

The United States of America was formed as a new country in 1776. There were many important people and events that helped to make that happen. A new country required a new government so that people knew the rules. Two very important documents were written around this time. Both of these documents still influence life today in America.

The first is the Declaration of Independence. This document officially declared the colonies free from Great Britain. It was written by Thomas Jefferson and signed by 56 delegates on July 4, 1776. It is one of the most famous documents in the world.

The second important document is the United States Constitution. It came after America was independent. Rather than declaring independence, this document is the basic set of laws for our nation. It contains rules for writing and passing laws. A group of 55 delegates contributed to writing this document in 1787.

These two documents are some of the most important papers in the whole world. They were written for two very different purposes. Yet both are over 300 years old and still influence how the United States operates today.

❶ What are two things that the Declaration of Independence and the United States Constitution have in common?

a. _____

b. _____

❷ What are two things that are different about these two famous documents?

a. _____

b. _____

Name:_____ Date: _____

Make Your Own Comparisons

Directions: Choose two informational texts about the same topic. Complete the Venn diagram to show how they are similar and different.

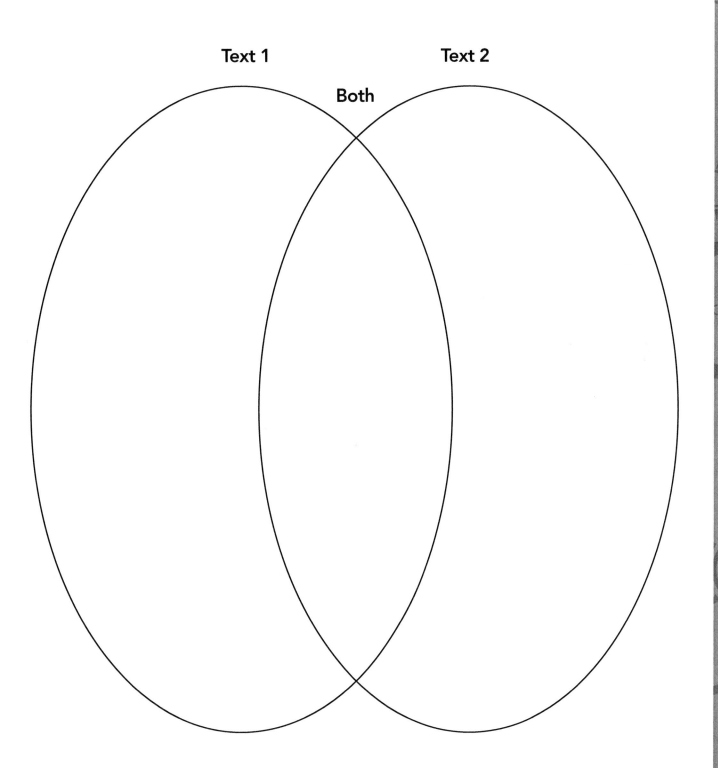

Text 1   Both   Text 2

Name:_____ Date: _____

Solving Problems

. . . .

Directions: Read the examples of problems that could be found in informational texts. Think about solutions to the problems. Write as many ideas as you can.

Problem: Our climate is changing. Air pollution and other man-made problems are warming the planet. Arctic ice is melting very quickly. Yet, polar bears need to walk on the ice to find food.

Solution(s): _____

_____

_____

_____

_____

Problem: Professional sports teams are more competitive than ever. Athletes feel pressure to perform to higher levels than ever before. More athletes are testing positive for using illegal performace drugs. These help their bodies do amazing things in competitions, but they are illegal.

Solution(s): _____

_____

_____

_____

_____

Problem: People living in regions that are part of "Tornado Alley" should pay attention to warnings and watches for these types of violent storms. These dangerous, spinning funnel clouds cause a lot of damage and put the lives of people in their paths in danger.

Solution(s): _____

_____

_____

_____

_____

Name: _____ Date: _____

Solutions in Editorials

An **editorial** is a type of informational text. It is a persuasive essay written by the editor of a newspaper or magazine. The content of an editorial deals with topics that are important to the audience of the publication.

Directions: Read the following editorial and answer the questions.

Healthy Food, Unhealthy Waste

The cafeteria at Willow Elementary is a busy place. It serves over 400 students. In recent years, the school district has worked hard to create a healthy and nutritious menu. Everyone is thrilled with this new development.

However, one problem remains in the cafeteria that has not been addressed. Students are eating these healthy foods off Styrofoam trays that are not recyclable. They are using plastic utensils that go straight into the garbage. This wasteful practice seems to contradict the healthy menu served each day. If we can't keep our planet clean, why does it matter to feed our bodies good food?

There are alternatives to this problem. Recyclable trays and utensils could be used. They are more expensive, but isn't it worth it?

1 What is the problem described in this editorial?

_____

_____

2 Why do you think this issue is important to consider?

_____

_____

Name:_____ Date: _____

Problem/Solution Patterns in Texts

Directions: Choose an editorial or other type of text that includes a problem/solution structure. Summarize the content of the text by filling out the graphic organizer.

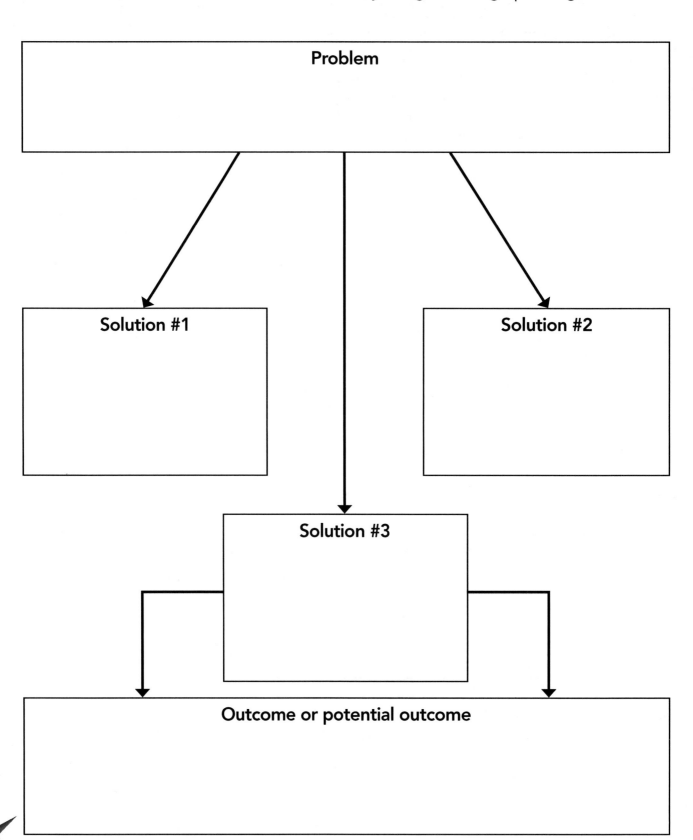

Problem

Solution #1

Solution #2

Solution #3

Outcome or potential outcome

Name: _____ Date: _____

Firsthand Versus Secondhand Accounts

A historical event in an informational text may be told from different perspectives.

A **firsthand account** is shared by an original source, someone who is or was a witness to the event being described.

A **secondhand account** is shared by somebody other than an original source, a person who was not at the actual event.

Directions: Read the text below and on the next page. Then, answer the questions.

Tecumseh: I Am a Shawnee

"It is true I am a Shawnee. My forefathers were warriors. Their son is a warrior. From them I take only my existence; from my tribe I take nothing. I am the maker of my own fortune; and oh! That I could make of my own fortune; and oh! That I could make that of my red people, and of my country, as great as the conceptions of my mind, when I think of the Spirit that rules the universe. I would not then come to Governor Harrison to ask him to tear the treaty and to obliterate the landmark; but I would say to him: Sir, you have liberty to return to your own country.

The being within, communing with past ages, tells me that once, nor until lately, there was no white man on this continent; that it then all belonged to red men, children of the same parents, placed on it by the Great Spirit that made them, to keep it, to traverse it, to enjoy its productions, and to fill it with the same race, once a happy race, since made miserable by the white people, who are never contented but always encroaching. The way, and the only way to check and to stop this evil is for all the red men to unite in claiming a common and equal right in the land, as it was at first, and should be yet; for it never was divided, but belongs to all for the use of each. For no part has a right to sell, even to each other, much less to strangers—those who want all, and will not do with less.

Firsthand Versus Secondhand Accounts *(cont.)*

The white people have no right to take the land from the Indians, because they had it first; it is theirs. They may sell, but all must join. Any sale not made by all is not valid. The late sale is bad. It was made by a part only. Parts do not know how to sell. All red men have equal rights to the unoccupied land. The right of occupancy is as good in one place as in another. There cannot be two occupations in the same place. The first excludes all others. It is not so in hunting or traveling; for there the same ground will serve many, as they may follow each other all day; but the camp is stationary, and that is occupancy. It belongs to the first who sits down on his blanket or skins which he has thrown upon the ground; and till he leaves it no other has a right."

❶ This is a firsthand account of an Indian who does not believe the Indians should be giving up their land to the government. How did this account make you feel as you were reading it?

_____

_____

❷ How did the personal language of this account affect the message he was trying to deliver?

_____

_____

Directions: Read a secondhand account of the situation. Then, answer the questions on the following page.

Battle of Tippecanoe

At the end of the 18th century, treaties were signed by some Indian leaders that gave up much of the land in present-day Ohio. This was an area that had been long inhabited by the Shawnee Indians, as well as other tribes. William Henry Harrison was the governor of the newly formed Indiana Territory. Harrison was interested in larger American expansion and wanted more land for white settlers. Tecumseh, a leader of the Shawnee, opposed this expansion.

Firsthand Versus Secondhand Accounts *(cont.)*

In 1810, the American Indian confederacy continued to fight efforts of the United States to take over land that the government believed to be their own. Tecumseh was outraged that treaties were still being signed by other tribes that gave away Indian land. Talks between the two sides failed, as tensions began to rise. This resulted in the Battle of Tippecanoe, in which the Indian warriors lost to Harrison's army.

3 What are the main differences between the two versions?

_____
_____
_____
_____

4 What are the similarities between the two versions?

_____
_____
_____
_____

5 Why might a reader's understanding and reaction to a firsthand account be different from the reaction to a secondhand account?

_____
_____
_____
_____

6 What type of event might be better written as a secondhand account?

_____
_____
_____
_____

Name:_____ Date: _____

Learning from Charts

A **chart** is a way to organize and display information.

Directions: A table is a type of chart. Read the table below. It is taken from an informational text about rocks and geology. Use the table to answer the questions.

Three Major Classifications of Rocks			
Classification	rock	color	structure
Igneous Rock (forms from hardened magma)	granite	white to gray, pink to red	closely arranged medium-to-coarse crystals
	obsidian	black, sometimes with brown streaks	glassy, no crystals
	pumice	grayish-white	light, fine pores, floats on water
Sedimentary Rock (formed by hardening of plant, animal, and mineral materials)	coal	shiny to dull black	brittle, in seams of layers
	limestone	white, gray, and buff to black and red	dense, forms cliffs, and may contain fossils
	shale	yellow, red, gray, green, black	dense, fine particles, soft, smells like clay
Metamorphic Rock (formed by existing rock changing because of heat or pressure)	marble	many colors, often mixed	medium-to-coarse crystals
	quartzite	white, gray, pink, and buff	big, hard, and often glassy
	schist	white, gray, red, green, black	flaky, banded, sparkles with mica

Learning from Charts *(cont.)*

1 What is the name of the igneous rock that is black and has a glassy appearance?

_____

2 What classification of rock is most likely to contain fossils?

_____

_____

3 Why do you think the author put the information in a table, instead of explaining it in a paragraph?

_____

_____

_____

_____

_____

_____

_____

_____

4 What are reasons for using a table in an informational text?

_____

_____

_____

_____

_____

_____

_____

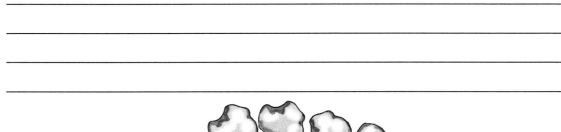

Name:_____ Date: _____

Interpreting Charts on Your Own

Directions: Locate a chart in an informational text that you are reading. Study the chart and read the text that goes with it. Then, answer the questions.

Title: _____

Author: _____

Topic: _____

1 Explain what the chart looks like and what information it displays.

_____

_____

_____

2 How does the chart help you understand the topic?

_____

_____

_____

3 Does the chart make your reading more interesting? Why or why not?

_____

_____

_____

4 List three questions you can answer by studying the chart.

_____

_____

_____

_____

_____

Name: _____ Date: _____

Understanding Graphs in Informational Texts

Graphs are visual representations of data. Graphs organize and display information to show the relationship between two or more quantities.

Directions: Read this excerpt from an informational text. Study the graph that is shown with the text. Then, answer the questions on the following page.

Planting a Garden

Landscape designers will plan for all types of materials in an outdoor space. They are responsible for combining all the components of a yard and arranging them in ways that make sense and maximize use for the residents. Swimming pools, patios, fences, lawns, and gardens are all elements that a landscape designer may suggest for a newly renovated backyard.

One aspect of a yard that many people enjoy is a fruit or vegetable garden. Finding the right spot for a garden is key since access to sunlight and a water source are essential. Choosing what to grow and when to plant seeds also requires some careful thought. This chart shows how long it takes before some vegetables are ready to harvest.

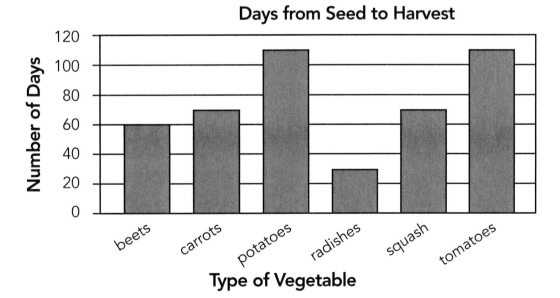

Days from Seed to Harvest

Understanding Graphs in
Informational Texts *(cont.)*

1 How long does it take carrots to grow?

_____

2 Which vegetables should be planted first to make sure they have enough time to grow?

_____

3 If you are reading this text about landscape design, how might this graph help you better understand this topic?

_____

_____

_____

_____

_____

_____

4 Why might it be better to present this information as a graph, rather than simply explaining it in a paragraph?

_____

_____

_____

_____

_____

_____

Name: _____ Date: _____

Reading Diagrams

A **diagram** is picture that is labeled so that a reader can easily learn parts of what is pictured. It is a good way to present information visually to help the reader understand information.

Directions: Read the text below and study the diagram. Then, answer the questions on the following page.

Ant Colonies

Ants are amazing, hard-working creatures. They live in large groups in underground colonies where they eat and mate. Colonies are built by the ants themselves and are quite sophisticated, with different "rooms" for storing food, taking care of babies, and serving other functions.

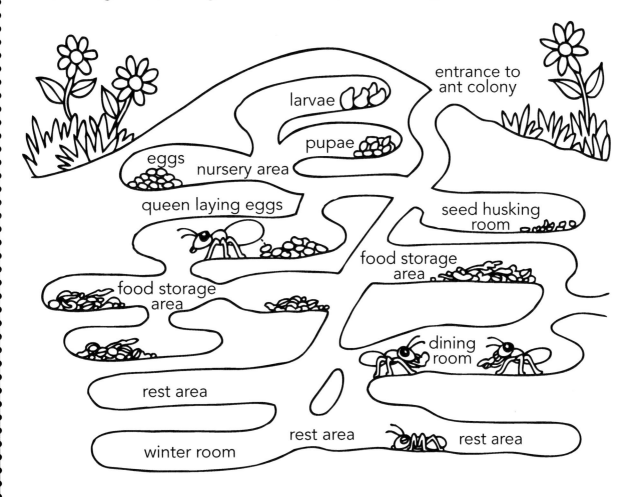

Reading Diagrams *(cont.)*

1 What are some of the special areas of the ant colony?

_____

_____

_____

_____

2 What words would you use to describe ants as a species?

_____

_____

_____

_____

_____

_____

3 How does the diagram help you understand more about how ants behave and work?

_____

_____

_____

_____

_____

_____

_____

_____

_____

_____

Name:_____ Date: _____

Understanding Timelines

A **timeline** is a visual map that shows events that happened in the order they happened. You read timelines from left to right. A timeline helps you easily see what happens over an extended period of time.

Directions: Study the following timeline for George Washington, the first president of the United States. Use it to answer the questions.

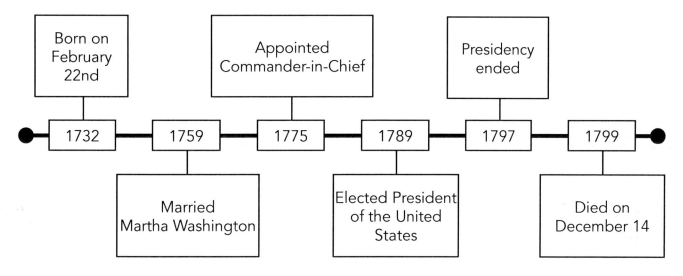

1 What year was George Washington born?

_____

2 How old was he when he died?

_____

3 How long was he president of the United States?

_____

4 How is this timeline helpful in understanding George Washington and his life?

_____

_____

_____

_____

Name:_____ Date: _____

Mapping Out a Timeline

Directions: Look at the blank timeline below. Choose the most important events from your own life to represent on a timeline. Put them in order and label the timeline. Make sure to write a description of each event and a date.

Directions: Use the information you placed on the timeline to write a short chronological account of your life.

_____
_____
_____
_____
_____
_____
_____
_____
_____
_____
_____
_____
_____
_____
_____
_____

Name:_____ Date: _____

An Author's Use of Evidence

Directions: Read the text below and on the next page. Underline each of the author's claims, or main points. Then, circle all evidence the author includes to support each claim. Finally, answer the questions on the next page.

Dear Restaurant Manager:

Though I have enjoyed your food in the past, I believe that the quality of your business has suffered recently and that certain issues demand your prompt attention. Recently, I was in your pizzeria and was extremely disappointed in the service that I received. On September 20th, I arrived with my family for dinner and was told that we should expect to wait about 30 minutes. More than 60 minutes passed before we were seated, and no one apologized for this inconvenience. This is unacceptable!

Our table was dirty when we sat down, and our waitress did not immediately clean it up. Though she took our order promptly, we waited more than 20 minutes for drinks and appetizers to arrive. When the food arrived, the order was wrong! The waitress did not seem to be too concerned, and in fact was quite rude when we asked for the items that we ordered.

By this time, we were ready to leave, but all four of us were starving and we knew that we had loved your pizza in the past. What happened to it? The pizza arrived and was not even cooked all the way through. The crust was soggy, and the toppings did not even taste right. It was the worst pizza I have ever had.

We were very surprised to see that your customer service has suffered so horribly. There was no mention of taking things off our bill, no visit by the manager, not even a thank you. I like to support local businesses, but I can't spend money on restaurant experiences such as this one.

Please check into this matter immediately and do what you can to change your customers' experiences. We want to be loyal customers, but we need to see some sign of improvement first before we will visit your pizzeria for a future meal.

Sincerely,

Fred Gandley

An Author's Use of Evidence (cont.)

1 Were all claims supported by sufficient, credible evidence? Explain.

_____

_____

_____

_____

2 Did the claims effectively support the author's position on the topic? Explain.

_____

_____

_____

_____

3 Overall, was the argument effective? Do you think the restaurant manager will change his actions? Explain.

_____

_____

_____

_____

Name:_____ Date: _____

Where's the Evidence?

Directions: Choose an informational text. Read the author's argument carefully. Then, complete the chart below.

| Title: _____ |
| Author: _____ |
| Topic or Main Idea: _____ |

	Well Done	Acceptable	Unacceptable
The author's position is clearly stated.			
The author makes claims to support the position.			
The author's claims are supported by evidence.			
The evidence is sufficient to support the claims.			

Name:_____ Date: _____

Word Sleuths: Finding Context Clues

A **context clue** is a word or phrase within a text that helps a reader understand an unfamiliar word. The following are some main types of context clues.

Direct Definition: The meaning of the word is clearly identified and often set off by a comma or set of commas.

The police officer had to <u>verify</u>, or confirm, the person's identification.

Synonyms: A synonym is included near an unfamiliar word to help explain its definition.

I tried to <u>skim</u> the ingredient list. I didn't have time to read it very closely.

Antonyms: An antonym is included to provide a clue about meaning.

My mom thought it was certainly <u>plausible</u> that the dog had eaten my homework, but my dad knew it was not believable.

Directions: Write which type of clue is found within the sentence or sentences. The focus vocabulary words are in italics.

1 Greta's teacher is quick to share *criticism* with her students. They wish she gave them more praise instead.

_____

2 Recycling is a *fundamental*, or basic, way to help the environment.

_____

3 Mrs. Anders felt that rules for good manners in line were *implicit*. The students understood the rules even though they were never stated clearly.

_____

Name:_____ Date: _____

Synonyms or Antonyms: Using Context Clues

Directions: Read the sentences. They include synonym or antonym context clues. Look at each word in italics and write its definition on the line provided.

1 The boss *assumed* that his employee took money from the safe. He thought it was true even though he had no evidence to think so.

_____

2 The art museum did not have a lot of *diverse* activities. It only focused on watercolors rather than including many different kinds of materials.

_____

3 We could not *discern* between the two dogs that were both brown with white spots because it was hard to distinguish between two dogs that looked so similar.

_____

4 Bringing up dinosaurs in a discussion about today's endangered animals is not *relevant* because the two topics are unrelated.

_____

5 My mom told me we will find out who the mystery person is at the *conclusion* of the story. She said this was just the beginning of the tale!

_____

6 I wish that I had *anticipated* this rainy weather. I was not thinking ahead and forgot my rain boots.

_____

7 Rowan wanted to be the helper who *compiled* the posters from different classrooms, but her partner Chloe wanted to distribute them and they couldn't agree.

_____

8 Jessie hoped to give an *eloquent* speech for school president, but instead her nerves got the best of her and she was quiet, shy, and forgot part of her speech.

_____

Name:_____ Date: _____

Explanations and Examples: Unraveling Clues in Context

· ·

Directions: Read the sentences. They include synonym or antonym context clues. Look at each word in italics and write its definition on the line provided.

1 My card was *invalid*, or void and cancelled, because it had expired the month before our trip.

_____

2 Uncle Arthur's cancer followed a slow but steady *progression*. It first began as a small lump, then gradually changed to a bigger lump, before advancing to a painful ache in his chest.

_____

3 The coach who *preceded*, or went before, my current coach was much tougher on the players and made them run laps as punishment.

_____

4 The reader enjoyed the *suspense* in the final chapters of the book. She liked that feeling of tense excitement about how something might turn out.

_____

5 My dance teacher decided to *improvise* one of our lessons. She could tell that the group needed to move on to something different, so she substituted her plans and made a quick decision to change the lesson.

_____

6 The *ideology*, or philosophy, that believes children should have time for imaginary play is something I agree very strongly with for many reasons.

_____

7 Our class would always *erupt*, or break out, in laughter whenever Shannon raised her hand because she was the class clown.

_____

Name:_____ Date: _____

Tracking Context Clues

Directions: Look for context clues in the books and texts that you read. Keep track of clues that you find that help you learn new words.

Word definition			
Type of clue			
Context clue			
Vocabulary word			

Name:_____ Date:_____

The Root of the Word

A **root word** contains the core meaning of the word, but it can't always stand alone. A **prefix** is at the beginning of a word, and a **suffix** is at the end of a word. These word parts change the meaning of the root word.

Directions: Divide the words into roots, prefixes, and suffixes in the spaces provided. Not every word will have all three parts.

Word	Prefix	Root	Suffix
1 import	im	port	———
2 prepay			
3 likeable			
4 loyalty			
5 autopilot			
6 telegram			
7 biology			
8 nonstop			
9 international			
10 telephone			

Name:_____ Date: _____

Root for the Word!

Directions: Use the Word Part definitions to help you write possible definitions for the listed vocabulary words.

Latin Word Parts

Prefixes	Root words	Suffixes
de-: away, off	*-dict-*: to say	*-able*: capable or worthy of
inter-: between, among	*-ject-*: to throw	*-fy*: to make or cause to become
trans-: across or over	*-port-*: to carry	*-ian*: related to, one that is
sub-: under	*-scrib- or -script-*: to write	

Greek Word Parts

Prefixes	Root words	Suffixes
bio-: life	*-chron-*: time	*-gram*: something written or drawn
geo-: Earth	*-path-*: feeling, suffering	*-graph*: something written or drawn
pan-: all	*-phon-*: sound	*-logy*: the study of

1 geology _____

2 transcribe _____

3 interject _____

4 deport_____

5 subway _____

6 biology _____

Name: _____ Date: _____

Grouping Together the Word Parts

Directions: Look at the words. Think of other words that have the same word parts (prefixes, roots, or suffixes) and write them in the boxes.

biology	disrespect
transport	describe
geography	microscope
telegraph	kilometer

Name: _____ Date: _____

Adding on to the Root

Directions: Use the root word part provided to complete each sentence.

1 Mr. Walters asked his students to make sure to include character _____ (-*logue*) in their narrative stories.

2 The piano is not very _____ (-*able*) because it is too heavy for one person to move it easily.

3 After the game, the baseball fan asked the pitcher for his _____ (-*graph*) on the foul ball that the fan caught during the eighth inning.

4 A _____ (*geo-*) came to our classroom to talk about his job studying rocks and the earth.

5 The scientist decided to use the _____ (*micro-*) to study small bacteria and learn more about it.

6 Workers take the _____ (*sub-*) to work so that they don't have to drive their own cars.

Name:_____ Date:_____

Using a Dictionary

A **dictionary** is a reference book that contains words listed in alphabetical order and gives explanations of their meanings. It often will include information about grammar, pronunciation, and other facts about the words.

Directions: Choose two words from the dictionary. Fill out the lines below with the information that you find in the dictionary.

Vocabulary word: _____
Guide words: _____
Relevant definition: _____
Definition in your own words: _____ _____
Pronunciation: _____
Part of speech: _____

Vocabulary word: _____
Guide words: _____
Relevant definition: _____
Definition in your own words: _____ _____
Pronunciation: _____
Part of speech: _____

Name: _____ Date: _____

Support Your Writing with a Dictionary

Directions: Read each of the challenging vocabulary words. Look up each word and learn its definition. Then, write a sentence that uses the word correctly.

1 *eligible*

_____

_____

_____

2 *civic*

_____

_____

_____

3 *enhance*

_____

_____

_____

4 *hoax*

_____

_____

_____

5 *exploit*

_____

_____

_____

6 *makeshift*

_____

_____

_____

Name:_____ Date: _____

New Words in the Thesaurus

A **thesaurus** is a reference book that lists words related to each other in meaning. It usually gives synonyms (words that mean the same) and antonyms (words that mean the opposite).

Directions: Look up the words in a thesaurus and write words or phrases that mean the same as the word.

1 *genre*

_____

_____

2 *loathe*

_____

_____

3 *futile*

_____

_____

4 *inept*

_____

_____

5 *discretion*

_____

_____

6 *commend*

_____

_____

Name: _____ Date: _____

As Smart as a What? Identifying Similes

A **simile** is a way to compare two different things, using the words *like* or *as* to show how the items are alike.

Example: Her teeth were *as* white *as* winter snow.

Directions: Try to explain the comparisons in the following similes.

1 The baseball whizzed by like a rocket.

The baseball _____ and a rocket _____.

2 The doctor's hands were as cold as ice.

The doctor's hands are _____ and ice is _____.

3 The athlete is as strong as an ox.

The athlete is _____ and an ox is _____.

4 The baby's body smells fresh as a flower.

The baby's smell is _____ and a flower's smell is

_____.

5 The little girl's eyes were bright like diamonds.

The little girl's eyes are _____ and a diamond is

_____.

Directions: Rewrite these sentences using a simile to make them more descriptive and interesting.

6 She slept after a long day.

_____

_____

7 During the test, the class was still.

_____

_____

Name:_____ Date: _____

Comparison Writing with Similes

. . . .

Directions: Look at the pairs of words. Use each pair to write a simile.

1 *grass, shirt*

_____

_____

_____

2 *boat, hummingbird*

_____

_____

_____

3 *eyes, sunset*

_____

_____

_____

4 *children, bees*

_____

_____

_____

5 *hurricane, soldier*

_____

_____

_____

6 *whale, pirate ship*

_____

_____

_____

Name:_____ Date: _____

Vivid Descriptions with Metaphors

A **metaphor** is a way to compare different things. Unlike a simile, metaphors do not use the words *like* or *as*. Metaphors help an author paint a vivid mental picture for the reader.

Example: *The books were a row of dominoes, toppling off the shelf.*

Directions: Create metaphors using one word from Group One and one word from Group Two.

Group One		Group Two	
love	pizza	jail	a trophy
money	anger	a dark cloud	music
summertime	dreams	freedom	an ocean
school	wrinkles	a vacation	a race
friends		a best friend	

1 _____

_____

2 _____

_____

3 _____

_____

4 _____

_____

Name: _____ Date: _____

Emotional Metaphors:
Comparing Emotions to Many Things

Metaphors may compare one thing in several different ways. Read the ways in which friendship is described using metaphors.

Friendship is a special treasure that should be carefully guarded.

Friendship is a roller coaster ride with ups and downs.

Friendship is a rope that makes you feel tied to another person.

Directions: Write comparisons for the following emotions.

Surprise is _____

_____

_____

Sadness is _____

_____

_____

Pride is _____

_____

_____

Fear is _____

_____

_____

Name:_____ Date: _____

What's That Idiom?

An **idiom** is a group of words whose meaning differs from the actual words being used.

Example: I mowed the yard and weeded the garden, <u>killing two birds with one stone</u>. (Translation: I accomplished two things at once.)

Directions: Match the idioms to the definitions on the right.

Idioms	Definitions
1 born with a silver spoon in his mouth	**a.** become very angry
2 walking on air	**b.** extremely happy
3 leave no stone unturned	**c.** to have everything you want
4 though thick and thin	**d.** raining hard
5 hold your horses	**e.** to be very thorough
6 spill the beans	**f.** help me
7 hit the ceiling	**g.** tell a secret
8 pain in the neck	**h.** annoying person or thing
9 lend me a hand	**i.** wait patiently
10 raining cats and dogs	**j.** to stand by in good times and in bad

Name: _____ Date: _____

Writing with Idioms

· ·

Directions: Write a sentence and include the idiom in an appropriate way.

1 spill the beans

_____

_____

_____

2 in the doghouse

_____

_____

_____

3 shaking in your boots

_____

_____

_____

4 blow off steam

_____

_____

_____

5 pain in the neck

_____

_____

_____

6 lend me a hand

_____

_____

_____

Name:_____ Date: _____

Listen to that Old Adage

An **adage** is a short but memorable saying that shares an experience considered to be true by many people. It is often shared with others as advice or a warning.

Example: Don't count your chickens before they hatch.
(*Translation:* You can hope that certain things happen in the future, but you don't know for sure that they will actually happen.)

Directions: Read the adages. Write in your own words what they mean.

1 Look before you leap.

_____

_____

_____

2 Don't judge a book by its cover.

_____

_____

_____

3 When it rains, it pours.

_____

_____

_____

4 Better late than never.

_____

_____

_____

5 Two heads are better than one.

_____

_____

_____

Name: _____ Date: _____

Passing on the Wisdom

Directions: Interview three people to find out what adage or idiom has been a good source of advice for them. Write about your interviews in the spaces below.

Interview Subject: _____

Favorite Adage or Idiom: _____

_____

What It Means: _____

_____

Why It's Important: _____

_____

Interview Subject: _____

Favorite Adage or Idiom: _____

_____

What It Means: _____

_____

Why It's Important: _____

_____

Interview Subject: _____

Favorite Adage or Idiom: _____

_____

What It Means: _____

_____

Why It's Important: _____

_____

Name:_____ Date: _____

Inferring From a Picture

Making an **inference** means to draw a conclusion based on given information. Some authors do not explain everything fully. They expect readers to "read between the lines."

Directions: Look at the picture. Think about what you notice that may be happening in this picture. Then, answer the questions.

❶ What are the kids doing? How do you know?

_____

_____

❷ Why are the kids facing each other?

_____

_____

❸ Why does the girl have her hands folded?

_____

_____

Name: _____ Date: _____

Explicit vs. Implicit Details

Sometimes making an inference is not necessary. The author includes **explicit** information that is very clear and easy to understand.

Other times, the details are not as clear and easy to recognize. They are **implicit.** A reader must make an inference about what is actually happening.

Directions: Decide whether each sentence group gives you explicit information or whether you have to make an inference based on implicit details. Write *explicit* or *implicit* on the lines provided.

1 The woman wore her new red dress to the fundraiser. She saw many friends that she knew and was excited to have a good time.

_____

2 Grace was ready for the bell to ring. She was so excited. Cake, balloons, presents, and dinner out at a restaurant—it was going to be a great night!

_____

3 Manuel only got halfway home on his bike. He was so frustrated. It was still a long walk. He took one more look at the tire and then just started walking, feeling sorry for himself.

_____

4 Many of the reasons that plants and animals are endangered are due to the actions of human beings. Pollution is one of the main reasons that living things are struggling to survive.

_____

5 It is Emily's favorite time to be outside and look up at the sky. The rain stops and the sun comes out. Then, as if a painter creates it in the sky, a beautiful scene emerges through the clouds.

_____

Explicit vs. Implicit Details *(cont.)*

6 Butterflies are beautiful insects. They flutter around in the spring air.

_____

7 Owning a pet is a huge responsibility. It is important to think about what type of animal is the best fit for the needs of your family.

_____

8 I can't believe that people can live in a place like this! It's hot all year long. There is very little rain. Besides, who thinks a cactus is beautiful? This place is awful.

_____

9 The car sped down the road. The cops were right behind it. The masked men in the car knew that a silent alarm had gone off in the bank. Why didn't they know about that alarm?

_____

10 Many holidays in the winter are celebrations that use light in some way. It is interesting to learn how different cultures all celebrate the dark, cold days of winter.

_____

Name:_____ Date: _____

Practice Making Inferences

Directions: Read the short paragraphs. Make an inference based on clues in the text and answer the questions.

"It sure is dark in here. Could we turn on some lights?" asked Wendy and Jack.

"The Fun House is too spooky!" said Jack as he walked through it.

"I'm ready to go on the Ferris wheel," said Wendy.

---

❶ What can you infer about what is happening?

_____

_____

❷ What clues did you find to prove you inferred correctly?

_____

_____

The sky was lit up with each boom. The crowd was in awe. It was the most spectacular show anyone had ever seen.

A warm summer night was the perfect setting for this light performance in the sky. How would they ever top this show next year?

---

❸ What can you infer about what is happening?

_____

_____

❹ What clues did you find to prove you inferred correctly?

_____

_____

Name: _____ Date: _____

Inferences in Text

Directions: Use this chart to record examples of inferences you may make in texts.

Clues you used to make inference	What it meant	Inference example	Title and author

Name:_____ Date: _____

Discovering the Theme

A **theme** is the central idea of a story. It is a lesson or message about life. The lesson might reflect something in your own life.

Directions: Read the text below and on the next page. Determine what the theme is, and write about it on the next page.

Nina's Day

Nina woke up on Friday with a plan. She knew she didn't want to go to school. Friday was always spelling test day, and this week she had forgotten to study. She had barely even looked at her spelling words, and now she was worried. She really didn't want to fail today's test.

So Nina hatched a plan. On Thursday night, she decided that she was going to play hooky. She was going to stay home from school. Of course, her parents were not aware of this plan. They woke up on Friday fully expecting Nina to get up, brush her teeth, eat breakfast, and catch the bus to school. So Nina knew that she had to be sneaky. She had to prove to them that she was sick, because that was the only way her mom and dad would ever allow her to stay home.

"Nina, time to get up!" her mother called.

"Mom, I'm sick. I woke up with a horrible stomachache," Nina lied.

After her mom talked to her, she was worried that Nina might actually be sick. "Well, I hate for you to miss school, but I really hate for you to go to school if you aren't feeling well. I'll call my boss and make sure it's okay that I stay home with you."

Nina couldn't believe it. Her plan had worked! A day home from school, and no spelling test! Hurray!

The morning was pretty uneventful. Nina got to watch a movie and stay on the couch. She felt pretty relaxed. Her mom was taking care of her. This was the best plan ever.

Discovering the Theme *(cont.)*

Later that afternoon, there was a knock on the door. Nina's mom opened it and saw that Sasha, Nina's best friend, was there.

"Hi Sasha, Nina can't play because she is sick today," said Nina's mother.

"I figured she must be sick because she wasn't in class today," Nina overheard Sasha tell her mom. "I'm sad we won't have our sleepover tonight."

"Sleepover? What sleepover?" wondered Nina. She had completely forgotten about her sleepover plans with Sasha, and now they were ruined. There was no way her mom would let her go after staying home sick.

"And I wanted to make sure to bring this gift book from the zoo. We got it on today's field trip. I thought that Nina might like to look at it. We sure missed her on today's trip. It was the best day of the school year so far!"

Nina's stomach started to hurt for real. She could not believe that she had forgotten that the spelling test had been canceled. She had missed the field trip to the zoo. Now she was missing a sleepover with her best friend.

This plan was not turning out the way she had hoped.

1 What is the theme of this story?

_____

_____

2 What evidence in the story helps you understand its theme?

_____

_____

_____

Name: _____ Date: _____

Comparing Themes To Experiences

A **theme** is the central idea of a story. It is a lesson or message about life. The lesson might reflect something in your own life.

Directions: Identify the theme of a text that you recently read. Consider how that theme relates to your own life. Use the chart below to share your ideas.

Title/Author: _____

Theme: _____

Evidence from the story	Experiences from your own life

Name:_____ Date: _____

Book Theme Graphic Organizer

A **theme** is the central idea of a story or text. It can be a lesson or a message about life.

Directions: Complete the graphic organizer to help you identify the theme of a literary work.

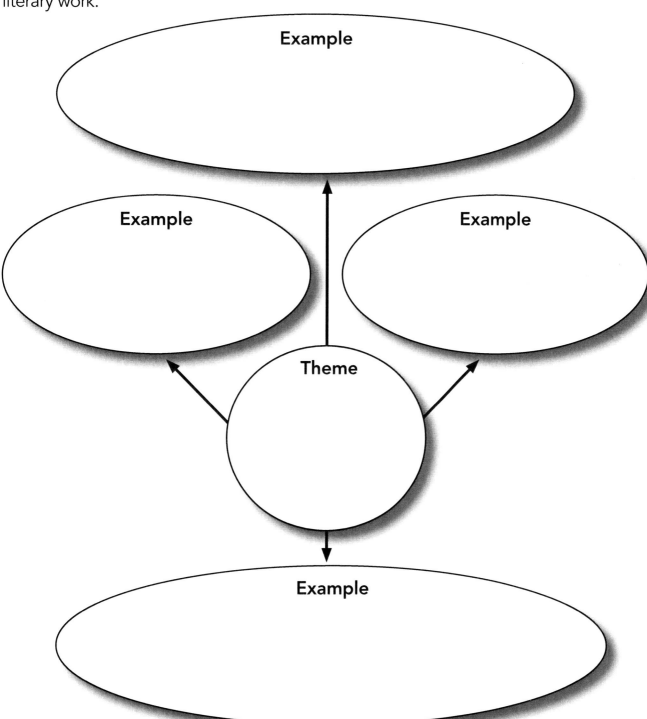

Name:_____ Date: _____

A Character Web

A **character** is a person (or animal, or imaginary creature) who takes part in the action of the story. Understanding a character's thoughts, words, and actions helps readers better understand the story itself.

Directions: Pick a character from a story. Fill out a character web. Write words or short phrases in the circles of the web. Add more circles if necessary.

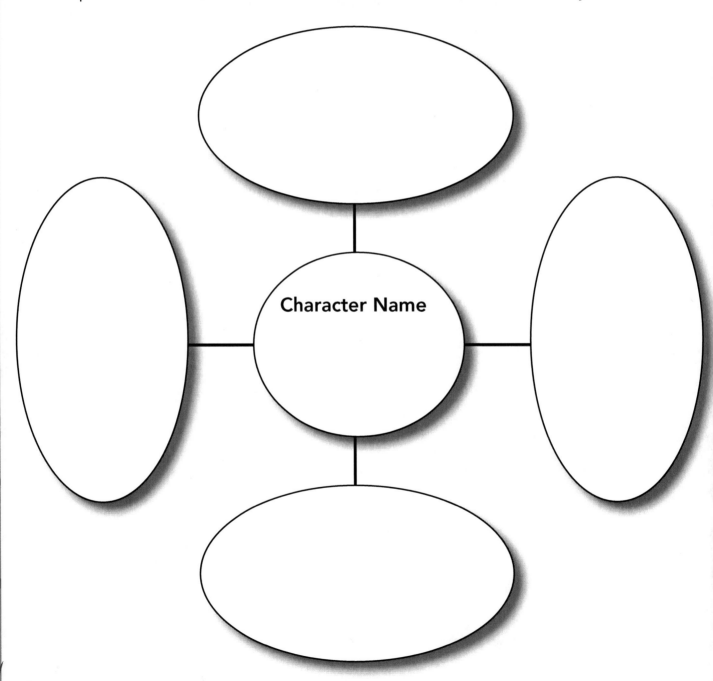

Character Name

Name: _____ Date: _____

Identifying Character Development

A **character** often changes throughout the course of a story. Some characters may learn an important lesson. Others may change from being bad to being good. Characters change as they respond to the conflicts in the story.

Directions: Pick a character that you know. Fill out the chart below to show how the character develops from the beginning to the end of the story.

Character Name: _____

	Beginning	Middle	End
Character's thoughts			
Character's words			
Character's actions			

Name:_____ Date: _____

Writing a Character Sketch

Directions: In paragraph form, write a character sketch that describes a character in a story. It may be a real character or one that you imagine.

Think about the following things when you write your sketch:

- What does your character look like?

- What does your character enjoy?

- Where does your character live?

- What does your character like to do?

- What are your character's struggles?

- What lessons does your character learn?

_____
_____
_____
_____
_____
_____
_____
_____
_____
_____
_____
_____
_____
_____
_____
_____
_____
_____
_____

Name:_____ Date: _____

Setting Survey

. . . .

A **setting** is an essential part of the story. It tells where and when the story takes place. It may be a real place or an imaginary, faraway land.

Directions: Choose a setting that you have read about in a story. Answer the questions below about this setting.

Title: _____

Author: _____

Setting: _____

❶ Describe the setting in detail.

_____

_____

_____

❷ How is this setting important to the story?

_____

_____

_____

_____

❸ How does the setting of the story change throughout the story?

_____

_____

_____

_____

Name:_____ Date: _____

Comparing Settings

Directions: Pick two stories and compare their settings. Use the Venn diagram below to list qualities about the setting that are similar and different.

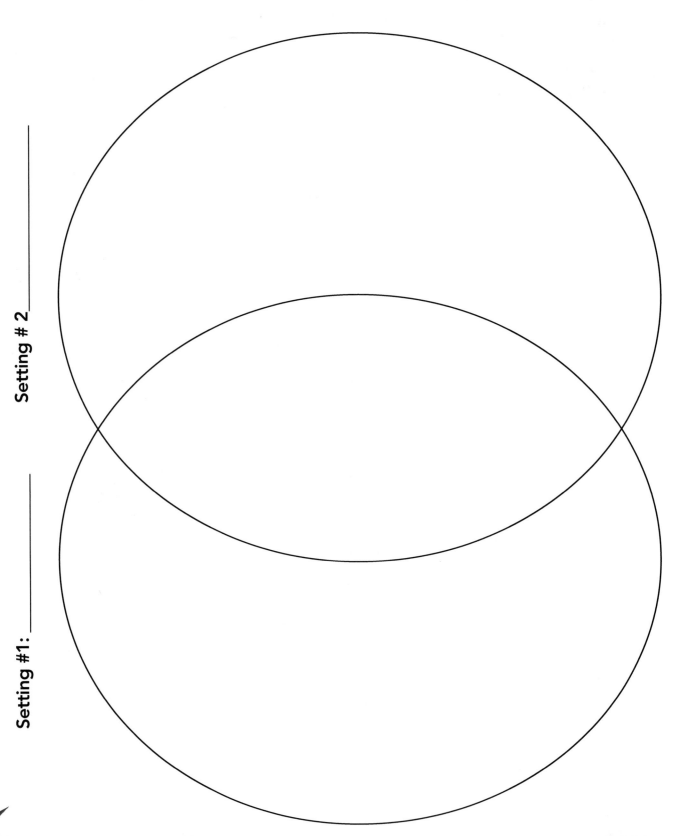

Setting # 2

Setting #1:

Name:_____ Date: _____

An Ideal Setting

Directions: What is the most perfect story setting that you can imagine? Write about it below, and then draw a picture to show what the setting looks like.

_____

_____

_____

_____

_____

Name: _____ Date: _____

Events That Build

An author carefully chooses how the events of a story unfold. The setting and the characters are critical to this, but the **plot** of the story is made up of a series of **events**. The order in which the events unfold is very important. In many stories, the events lead to the **climax.** This is the event with the greatest intensity, often when a great change occurs.

Directions: Choose a book. Think about the events of the book and how the events led up to the climax of the story. Record the events in the graphic organizer below.

Title: _____

Author: _____

Setting: _____

_____

_____

_____
Event 3

_____

_____
Event 2

_____

_____

_____
Event 1

Name: _____ Date: _____

Ordering Story Events

· ·

Directions: Think about a story that has events unfolding in a very specific order. Summarize the events in the chart below.

Events in a Story

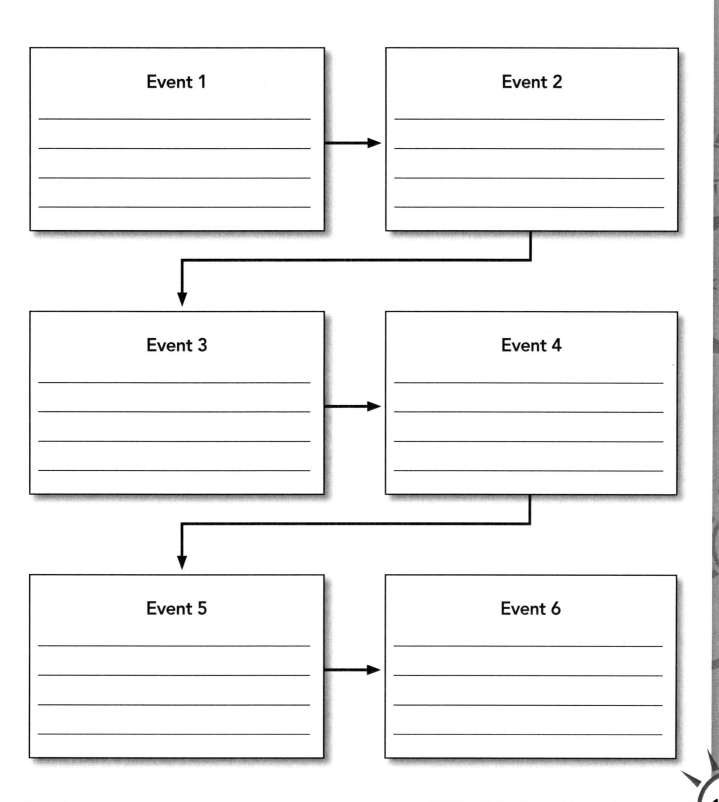

Name: _____ Date: _____

What Happens Next?

Directions: Look at the events listed below. They describe events from familiar stories. Write events that come before or after those listed.

The Three Little Pigs

Event #1	Event #2	Event #3
A wolf comes to the first house made of straw. He huffs and he puffs and he blows it down. He gobbles up the first little pig.	_____ _____ _____ _____ _____ _____	_____ _____ _____ _____ _____ _____

The Boy Who Cried Wolf

Event #1	Event #2	Event #3
_____ _____ _____ _____ _____	When others kept coming to rescue the boy, they saw that there was no wolf. People were frustrated that the boy had tricked them by calling "wolf."	_____ _____ _____ _____ _____

Name:_____ Date: _____

Descriptions from Mythology

Directions: Read the chart below to learn about people from ancient mythology. Then, answer the questions on the next page.

Name in Mythology	Title or quality	Example in today's language
Hercules	mighty and strong	A task that requires great strength or effort is considered to be a Herculean task.
Midas	turned everything he touched to gold	If someone has the Midas touch, then they have really good luck! Some use the expression to indicate that things come easily to a person.
Narcissus	beautiful human who fell in love with his own image	Narcissism means to have an exaggerated sense of how wonderful you are. It also means to have a big ego or to be conceited.
Pandora	the first woman who opened a box of evils	Opening a Pandora's box means to cause something bad to happen.

Descriptions from Mythology *(cont.)*

Directions: Use the examples and descriptions from ancient mythology to write about people in today's real world.

1 Hercules:

_____

_____

_____

_____

_____

2 Midas:

_____

_____

_____

_____

_____

3 Narcissus:

_____

_____

_____

_____

_____

4 Pandora:

_____

_____

_____

_____

_____

Name:_____ Date: _____

Analysis of a Hero or Heroine

Directions: Research three heroes or heroines from texts that you have read. Fill out the chart below based on what you learn about these great characters.

	Hero #1: _____	Hero #2: _____	Hero #3: _____
When did this person live?			
Where did this person live?			

Analysis of a Hero or Heroine *(cont.)*

	Hero #1: _____	Hero #2: _____	Hero #3: _____
Why is he or she a hero?			
Who considers this person to be a hero?			
What heroic qualities does this person have?			

Name:_____ Date: _____

A Different Point of View

Point of view is where the author "stands" when telling the story.

First Person Point of View: The author becomes the *I* in the story. In a first person story, one of the characters in the story tells it the way he or she saw it happen.

Third Person Point of View: An author can be on the sidelines of the story and report exactly what is seen and heard. In this case, the writer is like a reporter. The author uses *he* or *she*, instead of *I*.

Directions: Find examples of stories that you are reading or that you know that use either the first or third person points of view. Then, fill out the chart below.

	First Person Point of View
Title and Author	
Example from Text	
	Third Person Point of View
Title and Author	
Example from Text	

Name: _____ Date: _____

Changing Your Point of View

Directions: Consider how familiar stories might sound if told from a different point of view. Read the example and then write your own idea for the story suggestion.

Example: Cinderella from the point of view of a stepsister.

Unfair!

That dreaded Cinderella. She didn't deserve to go to the ball. Why should an ugly servant girl be allowed to go to such a special event? I was having a great time, and I know the prince was really enjoying my company. When a beautiful girl walked in and stole him away from me, I figured she was new to town. I would have never guessed that my awful stepsister would be the one to trick him into marrying her. I thought I would be able to trick him myself!

Write the Goldilocks tale from the point of view of the baby bear.

_____

_____

_____

_____

_____

_____

_____

_____

_____

_____

_____

_____

_____

Name:_____ Date: _____

Celebrating Around the World

Directions: Read this account of a family celebrating a holiday. Then, answer the questions on the next page.

Place Setting

In my family, Christmas Eve is more important than Christmas. We are Polish, and we follow Polish traditions. Actually, it is my grandmother, Babcia, who herds us outside for one of our first traditions. For the first time tonight, she leaves the kitchen, and we follow her into the quiet night.

We must see a star before we eat. All we see is a flicker—only an airplane. Our laughter fills the night. The first twinkle, high in the east, makes us smile. *Vigilea*, the vigil, waiting for Christmas, has begun.

We march inside, single file, to the table decorated in white. Candlesticks and a vase of holly nestle on hay, which resembles the manger and reminds us of the humble, quiet birth of Jesus. An extra place is set for the visitor who will join us in spirit at midnight. Before the food is served, the thin wafer we call *oplatek* (oh-PWAH-tek) is passed around the table from generation to generation. The wafer is shared as wishes of good health and happiness bond us.

Bowls of *borscht* (bawrsht), beet soup, are ladled into small china dishes. The magenta color is beautiful, and when a dollop of sour cream swirls through the steam on a silver spoon, the soup cools and thickens. Babka—light, flaky bread—is even more delicious with butter, and the stewed prunes and apricots sweeten the crusts of bread. Platters of fish and potato pancakes are emptied quickly, but Babcia's oven produces an endless supply to feed her family.

Celebrating Around the World *(cont.)*

Chrushchiki (khroos-CHEE-kee)—fried pastry with powdered sugar and a hint of cinnamon—disappears faster than the presents are opened on Christmas Day. *Koledy* (kol-YEN-da), or songs, are sung around Babcia's piano. Babcia remains in the kitchen, clearing and washing. She enjoys listening to our harmonious voices and knowing we are happy makes her happy.

When Babcia died, I realized how important Christmas Eve was. The first year, we all did something different. We had no shepherd to lead our flock. But this year, we have come together. I set two extra places at the dinner table. One is to remember Babcia.

1 How does this story remind you of how your own family celebrates a winter holiday?

_____

_____

_____

_____

2 What is different about how your family celebrates compared to how this family celebrates?

_____

_____

_____

_____

Name:_____ Date: _____

The Importance of Tradition

Directions: Read the tale from Russia. Then, answer the questions on the next page.

How the Sons Filled the Hut

In a small village, there was once a father who had three sons. Two were thought to be clever fellows, but the third was so simple everyone said the lad was a fool.

One day, the father decided to build a hut at the edge of his pasture. When the small house was finished, he called his sons together and said, "I will give this hut to the one who can fill it completely. Not even a corner is to be left empty."

The oldest son said, "I know the very thing that will do it."

And off he went to buy a horse. When he brought the animal into the new hut, the horse filled only one corner of the place.

At once, the second son hurried off, saying, "I know the very thing that will fill this hut." He returned with a load of hay, which he hauled into the new hut. The hay filled only half of the little house.

The youngest son scratched the top of his head with one hand. "I suppose it's my turn to try my luck," he said slowly, and then he trudged off into the village. There he wandered about for the rest of the day.

Toward evening, as the lights began to shine form the cottage window, the young lad suddenly slapped his thigh and laughed out loud. "Now I know the very thing that will do it!" he exclaimed.

Like a flash, he bought a fat candle and hurried to the new hut.

Once inside, the lad lit the candle—and lo—the whole hut was filled with light—every corner, nook, and cranny. And so the simple son, whom everyone thought was a fool, won the new little house for himself.

The Importance of Tradition *(cont.)*

1 What lesson(s) are told through this tale?

_____

_____

_____

_____

_____

_____

_____

_____

2 What other stories are you reminded of when you read this?

_____

_____

_____

_____

_____

_____

_____

_____

3 What did you learn about Russian culture from this story?

_____

_____

_____

_____

_____

_____

_____

_____

Name:_____ Date: _____

Common Themes Across Cultures

Directions: Look at the list below. Think about how these themes might be treated in different ways by different cultures. Look for a story that is representative of a different culture. Read it and then answer the questions.

Literature Themes

- Character is put to a test
- Character is changed into something better
- Character lives happily ever after
- Honesty or cleverness is rewarded
- Evil is punished
- Beauty is only skin deep
- Harmony with nature is important

1 What culture does this story represent?

_____

_____

_____

2 What does this story tell us about this culture?

_____

_____

_____

3 What stories does this tale remind you of?

_____

_____

_____

Fluency

Name:_____ Date: _____

Oral Reading Checklist

Directions: Use this checklist the next time you read aloud to rate your oral reading. You can rate yourself, or you can have someone else rate you.

Name of the story: _____

	Excellent	Satisfactory	Needs Work
Expression Expression is the way that you read words.			
Accuracy Accuracy is reading the words correctly.			
Pace Pace is the speed that you read. Was it too fast, too slow, or just right?			

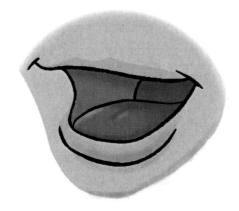

Name: _____ Date: _____

Timed Reading to Build Fluency

Directions: Use each chart to mark how much you read each time you are reading a text. Read the text at least three times.

Title of text: _____	
1st Reading	_____ words per minute
2nd Reading	_____ words per minute
3rd Reading	_____ words per minute

Title of text: _____	
1st Reading	_____ words per minute
2nd Reading	_____ words per minute
3rd Reading	_____ words per minute

Title of text: _____	
1st Reading	_____ words per minute
2nd Reading	_____ words per minute
3rd Reading	_____ words per minute

Writing

Name:_____ Date: _____

What's Your Opinion on That?

> An **opinion piece** is a way to share your own point of view in writing. Writers must support their views with facts and details.

Directions: Use this outline to plan an opinion piece.

Topic: _____

Central Point of View: _____

Opinion #1: _____

_____

Fact 1: _____

_____

Fact 2: _____

_____

Opinion #2: _____

_____

Fact 1: _____

_____

Fact 2: _____

_____

Opinion #3: _____

_____

Fact 1: _____

_____

Fact 2: _____

_____

Conclusion: _____

_____

Name: _____ Date: _____

All About Me: Writing to Inform

Directions: Pick a topic that helps describe something about yourself. Use the outline to help you organize your information.

Topic: _____

Introduction: _____

First Paragraph

Fact or Detail #1 _____

Fact or Detail #2 _____

Fact or Detail #3 _____

Second Paragraph

Fact or Detail #1 _____

Fact or Detail #2 _____

Fact or Detail #3 _____

Third Paragraph

Fact or Detail #1 _____

Fact or Detail #2 _____

Fact or Detail #3 _____

Conclusion: _____

_____

_____

_____

Name:_____ Date: _____

Putting All the Parts Together: Writing Narrative Stories

Narratives are stories. They can be true or make believe. Good stories have different parts.

Characters: the people or creatures in the story

Setting: the story's location

Problem: the problem in the story that may or may not be solved

Directions: Think about the order in which you want to write your story. This is called the sequence. Write about the sequence in the spaces below.

Beginning of the Story

_____

_____

_____

_____

_____

Middle of the Story

_____

_____

_____

_____

_____

End of the Story

_____

_____

_____

_____

Name: _____ Date: _____

Editing Checklist

Editing is an important part of the writing process. Going back to check for mistakes makes your writing stronger. It is helpful for any kind of writing assignment.

Directions: Use the checklist below when you are editing a piece of your writing. You can edit your own writing or a classmate's work.

- ❏ Write complete sentences

- ❏ Use correct capitalization

- ❏ Use quotation marks for dialogue

- ❏ Use end punctuation for sentences

- ❏ Choose descriptive words for effect

- ❏ Sequence the story in an order that makes sense

- ❏ Add story characters that are interesting and described well

- ❏ Describe a clear setting

- ❏ Vary sentence patterns for reader interest

- ❏ Check that subjects and verbs agree

- ❏ Include a conclusion that makes the story feel resolved and/or complete

Name:_____ Date: _____

Making the Most of Group Discussions

. . . .

Directions: Before, during, and after a whole-class or small-group discussion, complete this activity page to help you get the most out of the conversation.

Before Discussion

1 What information do you plan to share? Write down your ideas.

_____

_____

_____

_____

During Discussion

2 Listen carefully to each person's ideas. Use the space below to take notes.

_____

_____

_____

_____

After Discussion

3 What were the key parts of the discussion? Write down a few.

_____

_____

_____

_____

4 In your opinion, what was the main idea of the discussion?

_____

_____

_____

_____

Name:_____ Date: _____

Collaboration Includes Many Voices

Directions: Fill out this chart before, during, and after a group discussion.

The topic of the discussion: _____

Group member #1 _____	Group member #2 _____
Group member #3 _____	Group member #4 _____

What was the outcome of your group discussion?

_____

_____

_____

_____

_____

Name: _____ Date: _____

Comparing Quantities: Showing What Multiplication Means

A multiplication number sentence can be read as a comparison between the numbers in the equation.

$4 \times 4 = 16$

16 is the same as 4×4.

16 is the same as 4 times 4.

4×4 is the same as 16.

16 is the same as 4 sets of 4.

Directions: Draw pictures to represent the two quantities. Write two sentences to explain the comparisons.

❶ $3 \times 9 = 27$

_____

_____

❷ $5 \times 6 = 30$

_____

_____

Name:_____ Date: _____

Multiplication Equations

Directions: Solve the problems.

1 25 is the same as 5 times _____.

2 81 is the same as 9 times _____.

3 45 is the same as 5 times _____.

4 28 is the same as 4 times _____.

5 15 is the same as _____ times 3.

6 77 is the same as _____ times 7.

7 39 is the same as _____ times 3.

8 64 is the same as _____ times 8.

Directions: Solve the problems. You may include more than one answer.

9 40 is the same as:

_____ × _____

_____ × _____

_____ × _____

_____ × _____

10 100 is the same as:

_____ × _____

_____ × _____

_____ × _____

_____ × _____

11 12 is the same as:

_____ × _____

_____ × _____

_____ × _____

_____ × _____

12 36 is the same as:

_____ × _____

_____ × _____

_____ × _____

_____ × _____

Name:_____ Date: _____

Does Order Matter? The Commutative Property

The **Commutative Property of Multiplication** states that when the order of the factors is changed, the product stays the same.

$$5 \times 7 = 35$$

$$7 \times 5 = 35$$

Directions: Look at the numbers. Write two equations for each number that show the commutative property.

❶

_____ × _____ = 24

_____ × _____ = 24

❷

_____ × _____ = 72

_____ × _____ = 72

❸

_____ × _____ = 42

_____ × _____ = 42

❹

_____ × _____ = 56

_____ × _____ = 56

❺

_____ × _____ = 30

_____ × _____ = 30

❻

_____ × _____ = 12

_____ × _____ = 12

Name:_____ Date: _____

Using Operations to Solve Word Problems

Directions: Read the word problems. Write a number sentence and draw a picture to show your answer.

❶ Phoebe has to walk 8 blocks to school. Tony has to walk 2 times as many blocks. How many blocks does Tony walk to school?

Number Sentence: _____

Draw a picture.

❷ Jose scored 6 goals during the soccer game. He scored 2 times as many goals as Felix. How many goals did Felix score?

Number Sentence: _____

Draw a picture

Name:_____ Date: _____

As Much As What? Solving Word Problems

Directions: Solve the problems.

1 Amy has 3 books on her desk. Stacy has 7 times as many books as Amy. How many books does Stacy have?

Number Sentence: _____

Answer: _____

2 Jasper has 8 coins to buy a comic book. Elliot has 6 times as many coins as Jasper. How many coins does Elliot have?

Number Sentence: _____

Answer: _____

3 There are 24 bushes on the street. There are 6 times as many bushes as trees. How many trees are on the street?

Number Sentence: _____

Answer: _____

4 The student's desk is 36 inches long. The cafeteria table is 360 inches long. How many times longer is the table than the desk?

Number Sentence: _____

Answer: _____

Directions: Write a similar word problem. Trade it with a friend to solve.

Word Problem: _____

_____

_____

_____

_____

Number Sentence: _____

Answer: _____

Name:_____ Date: _____

Creating Math Stories

Directions: Write word problems to represent each equation.

1 $2 \times 20 = 40$

_____

_____

_____

_____

2 $8 \times 12 = 96$

_____

_____

_____

_____

3 $25 \times 4 = 100$

_____

_____

_____

_____

4 $3 \times 2 = 6$

_____

_____

_____

_____

5 $8 \times 8 = 64$

_____

_____

_____

_____

Name:_____ Date: _____

The Five-Step Plan

Use the **Five-Step Plan** to solve word problems.

❶ Read the problem. Make sure you understand the situation.

❷ State the problem to be solved.

❸ Determine the operation to be used. Do you need to add, subtract, multiply, or divide?

❹ Do the operations.

❺ Check the final answer to see if it is reasonable.

Directions: Use the Five-Step Plan. Use a separate sheet of paper if you need extra space.

Jack bought two toys at the store. Each toy cost 65 cents. He gave the cashier $2.00. How much change did he receive back from the cashier?

Step 1: Read the problem carefully.

Step 2: State the problem in your own words. _____

_____

Step 3: Determine the operations to be used.

The operations to be used are _____ .

Step 4: Do the operations.

Show your work in the space below.

Step 5: Check the final answer to see if it is reasonable.

Name:_____ Date: _____

A Little Bit of Everything: Multistep Word Problems

Directions: Read the word problems. You will need to do more than one step to solve each problem. Show the steps you take to find the final answer.

1 Sergio enjoys collecting stamps as a hobby. He collected 12 stamps in June, 24 in July, and 29 in August. Then, he decided to give 18 to his brother. How many stamps does Sergio have left?

2 Lily ate three strawberries at breakfast and had two times that many for lunch. If she wants to eat 20 strawberries in one day, how many will she need to have for dessert?

3 A large pizza has 24 slices. If 7 friends want to share the pizza, and they each want 3 slices, is there enough pizza? If so, how much is left?

4 Parker made 75 cents at his lemonade stand on Saturday. He made two times as much as that on Sunday. Parker wants to buy two candy bars that cost $1.00 each. Does he have enough money? If so, how much change will he get?

Name: _____ Date: _____

Solve That Letter: Unknown Quantities

Solving a problem may involve using letters for unknown quantities.

Example: $x - 4 = 6$

Guess and check! Substitute numbers for the quantity and see if you get the right answer.

To solve for x, you find out that $x = 10$.

Directions: Solve the problems. Explain your work and the steps you took to get an answer.

1 $y + 2 = 12$

How did you solve this problem? _____

_____

_____

_____

_____

2 $x + 6 = 15$

What steps did you take to solve this problem? _____

_____

_____

_____

_____

3 $x - 4 = 41$

What steps did you take to solve this problem? _____

_____

_____

_____

_____

Name:_____ Date: _____

Fun with Factor Pairs!

A **factor** is a number that divides exactly into another number. **Factor pairs** are two numbers multiplied together to get one number.

Factor pairs of 12 would be 12 and 1, 6 and 2, and 4 and 3.

Directions: Write all the factor pairs for the following numbers in the boxes.

1 30	**2** 24
3 16	**4** 42
5 88	**6** 50
7 66	**8** 72

Name:_____ Date: _____

Minding the Multiples

A **multiple** is the number resulting when any two factors are multiplied together. The multiple is the product of two factors.

In the equation 2 × 6 = 12, the number 12 is a multiple of 2 and 6.

Directions: Circle the correct multiple for each number.

1 12 15 18 is a multiple of 5.

2 24 22 28 is a multiple of 7.

3 30 35 39 is a multiple of 2.

4 52 64 69 is a multiple of 8.

5 81 87 93 is a multiple of 9.

6 84 86 98 is a multiple of 4.

7 52 30 59 is a multiple of 5.

8 62 38 18 is a multiple of 6.

Directions: List the first five multiples for each of the sets of numbers below.

9 10: _____, _____, _____, _____, _____

10 8: _____, _____, _____, _____, _____

11 6: _____, _____, _____, _____, _____

12 11: _____, _____, _____, _____, _____

Name:_____ Date: _____

Prime or Composite?

Composite numbers are numbers that can be divided up evenly and have factors other than themselves and 1.

Prime numbers are numbers that cannot be divided up evenly. They can only be divided by 1 and themselves.

The number 6 is a composite number. It can be divided evenly.

The number 7 is a prime number. It cannot be divided evenly.

Directions: Determine whether the numbers are prime or composite numbers.

1 8

2 17

3 25

4 31

5 37

6 42

Name:_____ Date: _____

More Prime or Composite?

A **factor tree** shows the prime factors of a composite number. Keep factoring a number until you only have prime numbers.

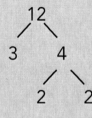

Directions: Use factor trees to determine the prime factors of these numbers.

1 44	**2** 36
3 100	**4** 63
5 18	**6** 72

Name:_____ Date: _____

What's the Rule?

Directions: Look at the number patterns. Add three more terms. Then, write the rule for each pattern.

1 7, 14, 21, 28, _____, _____, _____

Pattern Rule: _____

2 1, 4, 7, 10, _____, _____, _____

Pattern Rule: _____

3 1, 2, 5, 10, 17, _____, _____, _____

Pattern Rule: _____

4 63, 54, 45, 36, 27, _____, _____, _____

Pattern Rule: _____

5 1, 1, 2, 3, 5, 8, _____, _____, _____

Pattern Rule: _____

6 1, 3, 7, 13, 21, _____, _____, _____

Pattern Rule: _____

Directions: Write a pattern of your own. Leave the last two spaces blank. Trade papers with a friend and determine the rules.

Pattern #1: _____, _____, _____, _____, _____, _____

Pattern Rule: _____

Name: _____ Date: _____

Noticing Patterns in Numbers

Directions: Look at the number patterns. Add more terms. Then, write the rule and what you noticed about each pattern.

1 11, 22, 33, 44, _____, _____, _____, _____, _____, _____, _____

What is the rule for this pattern? _____

_____

What do you notice about this pattern?

_____

_____

_____

2 5, 10, 15, 20, _____, _____, _____, _____, _____, _____, _____

What is the rule for this pattern? _____

_____

What do you notice about this pattern?

_____

_____

_____

3 3, 6, 9, 12, _____, _____, _____, _____, _____, _____, _____

What is the rule for this pattern? _____

_____

What do you notice about this pattern?

_____

_____

_____

Name:_____ Date: _____

Patterns in Function Tables

Number patterns can be organized into a **function table**.

$x + 8 = y$		
x	equation	y
6	6 + 8 = y	14
8	8 + 8 = y	16
25	25 + 8 = y	33

The rule of this function table is to add 8 to a number. Each row of the table has an x number and a y number that go together in the equation.

Directions: Complete the function tables.

1

$x + 4 = y$		
x	equation	y
6		
8		
25		

3

$x \div 3 = y$		
x	equation	y
6		
45		
18		

2

$4x = y$		
x	equation	y
5		
9		
12		

4

$x - 20 = y$		
x	equation	y
40		
264		
59		

Name: _____ Date: _____

Expanded Form

Directions: Solve the problems.

❶ $624 \times 10 =$ _____

❷ $92 \times 100 =$ _____

❸ $43 \times 100 =$ _____

❹ $712 \times 10 =$ _____

Name:_____ Date: _____

Comparing the Places of Value

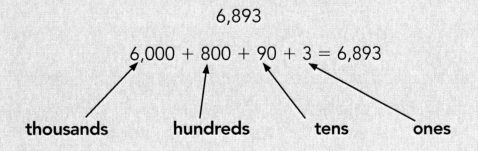

Place value refers to the value of the place that a digit occupies in a number.

$$6,893$$

$$6,000 + 800 + 90 + 3 = 6,893$$

thousands   hundreds   tens   ones

Directions: Solve the problems.

1 _____ thousands = 50 hundreds. Write the number. _____

2 _____ hundreds = 60 tens. Write the number. _____

3 _____ ones = 2 tens. Write the number. _____

4 _____ tens = 27 hundreds. Write the number. _____

5 _____ thousands = 356 hundreds. Write the number. _____

6 _____ ones = 87 tens. Write the number. _____

7 _____ ones = 91 tens. Write the number. _____

8 _____ thousands = 80 hundreds. Write the number. _____

Dividing the Places

$$850 \div 10 = 85$$
$$400 \div 100 = 4$$
$$25{,}000 \div 1{,}000 = 25$$

$$\begin{array}{r} 85 \\ 10\overline{)850} \\ -80 \\ \hline 50 \\ -50 \\ \hline 0 \end{array}$$

Directions: Solve the problems.

❶ 930 ÷ 10 = _____	❷ 1,000 ÷ 100 = _____
❸ 220 ÷ 10 = _____	❹ 6,700 ÷ 100 = _____
❺ 45,000 ÷ 1,000 = _____	❻ 90 ÷ 10 = _____

Name:_____ Date: _____

Fill in the Blank Values

Directions: Solve the problems.

1 _____ ÷ 10 = 450

2 100 × _____ = 8,200

3 300 ÷ 10 = _____

4 62 × _____ = 620

5 85,000 ÷ _____ = 85

6 770 ÷ _____ = 77

7 4 × _____ = 40

8 550 ÷ 10 = _____

9 1,800 ÷ 18 = _____

10 990 × _____ = 9,900

11 220 ÷ 10 = _____

12 12 × 100 = _____

13 2,000 ÷ _____ = 2

14 6 × _____ = 6,000

15 2,340 × _____ = 23,400

16 5,000 ÷ _____ = 50

Name: _____ Date: _____

Reading and Writing Numbers

Directions: Write each number using words.

1 1,001

_____

2 75

_____

3 621

_____

4 453

_____

5 33

_____

6 90

_____

7 2,056

_____

Directions: Read each number in word form. Then, write the number using digits.

8 six thousand fifty _____

9 two thousand eight hundred forty-two _____

10 eight thousand sixty-nine _____

11 one thousand five hundred _____

12 six thousand four hundred fifty-three _____

Name: _____ Date: _____

Expanding on Expanded Form

Directions: Write the numbers below using words.

1 6,000 + 400 + 70 + 6 = _____

_____

2 8,000 + 500 + 40 + 1 = _____

_____

3 2,000 + 900 + 50 + 9 = _____

_____

4 400 + 40 + 4 = _____

_____

5 1,000 + 80 + 2 = _____

_____

6 9,000 + 500 + 60 = _____

_____

7 3,000 + 90 + 9 = _____

_____

8 5,000 + 100 + 10 = _____

_____

Directions: Write the numbers below using digits.

9 8 thousands, 4 tens, and 3 ones

_____

10 8 thousands, 9 hundreds, 4 tens, and 3 ones

_____

11 3 thousands, 8 hundreds, 9 tens, and 3 ones

_____

12 1 thousand, 8 tens, and 3 ones

_____

Name:_____ Date: _____

Comparing Many Digits

Directions: Decide if the first number is greater, the same, or less than the second number. Use the >, =, < symbols to show your answers.

1 670 _____ 6,700

2 802 _____ 820

3 455 _____ 450

4 90 _____ 901

5 111 _____ 101

6 313 _____ 311

7 616 _____ 616

8 22 _____ 221

9 403 _____ 404

10 12 _____ 11

11 99 _____ 90

12 516 _____ 615

13 772 _____ 727

14 880 _____ 808

15 8,001 _____ 8,001

16 3,423 _____ 7,277

Name:_____ Date: _____

High Places to Low Places

Directions: Put the following groups of numbers in order from greatest to least.

❶ 310 _____

3,101 _____

3,100 _____

311 _____

❷ 660 _____

661 _____

6,600 _____

600 _____

❸ 70 _____

77 _____

700 _____

710 _____

❹ 444 _____

441 _____

4,400 _____

4,404 _____

❺ 55 _____

500 _____

505 _____

50 _____

❻ 111 _____

101 _____

110 _____

100 _____

Name:_____ Date: _____

Rounding Up and Rounding Down

··

> **Rounding** a number means changing a number to the nearest significant number above or below it.
>
> When rounding, use the following rules:
>
> - If the number is followed by a 5, 6, 7, 8, or 9, round the number up.
>
> - If the number is followed by a 0, 1, 2, 3, or 4, round the number down.

Directions: Round the numbers to the nearest ten.

1 86

_____

2 452

_____

3 91

_____

4 77

_____

5 293

_____

6 65

_____

7 313

_____

8 148

_____

Name:_____ Date: _____

What's A-Round 100?

Directions: Round the following numbers to the nearest hundred.

1 688

_____

2 314

_____

3 9,012

_____

4 8,229

_____

5 106

_____

6 2,888

_____

7 421

_____

8 1,345

_____

Directions: Round the numbers to the nearest hundred and estimate the answer.

9 120 + 120 = _____

10 504 + 671 = _____

11 8,199 + 133 = _____

12 150 + 260 = _____

13 1,230 + 1,110 = _____

14 985 + 756 = _____

Name:_____ Date: _____

A Thousand Times More Fun

. . . .

Directions: Round the numbers to the nearest thousand.

1 3,299

_____

2 8,876

_____

3 2,375

_____

4 10,333

_____

5 7,550

_____

6 4,505

_____

7 12,775

_____

8 6,543

_____

Directions: Round the numbers to the nearest thousand and estimate the answer.

8 4,566 – 2,990 = _____

9 67,988 – 38,403 = _____

10 9,330 ÷ 3,199 = _____

11 3,427 + 1,452 = _____

12 6,783 + 3,689 = _____

Name:_____ Date: _____

Round 'Em Up and Out!

Directions: Read the word problems and round the numbers according to the directions. Choose the letter that represents your answer.

1 The newspaper said about 496 people attended a horse show. If the newspaper were rounding to the nearest ten, about how many people attended the horse show?

    a. 550   **b.** 500   **c.** 489   **d.** 513

2 Our principal claims that she is responsible for 298 students. If she were rounding to the nearest ten, about how many students attend our school?

    a. 300   **b.** 280   **c.** 399   **d.** 210

3 Scientists claim that there are only about 5,400 birds of an endangered bird species left alive on Earth. If they are rounding to the nearest thousand, how many birds are left?

    a. 5,000   **b.** 5,330   **c.** 6,100   **d.** 4,500

4 Concert promoters say that 16,215 people attended the benefit show last night. If they are rounding to the nearest thousand, how many people attended the show?

    a. 16,901   **b.** 17,010   **c.** 16,210   **d.** 16,000

5 Round 21 to the nearest ten. Round 37 to the nearest ten. Multiply these two rounded numbers. What is the estimated answer?

    a. 90   **b.** 800   **c.** 1,000   **d.** 600

6 Round 190 to the nearest hundred. Round 510 to the nearest hundred. Add these two rounded numbers. What is the estimated answer?

    a. 750   **b.** 300   **c.** 10,000   **d.** 700

Name: _____ Date: _____

Steps to Addition

To find the sum of an addition problem, you have to use what you know about place value to solve the problem.

$$24$$
$$+ 62$$
$$86$$

↑ ↑
tens ones

Sometimes you have to regroup numbers.

$$\overset{1}{87}$$
$$+ 49$$
$$136$$

↑ ↑
tens ones

Directions: Solve the problems.

1
$$96$$
$$+ 56$$

2
$$39$$
$$+ 10$$

3
$$210$$
$$+ 400$$

4
$$390$$
$$+ 275$$

5
$$190$$
$$+ 78$$

6
$$208$$
$$+ 44$$

Name:_____ Date: _____

Taking More Steps to Add

Directions: Solve the problems.

1
```
  2,334
+    62
```

2
```
  24,860
+  9,540
```

3
```
  560
+  25
```

4
```
  30,877
+  5,398
```

5
```
  799
+ 108
```

6
```
  54,587
+ 12,488
```

7
```
  877
+ 200
```

8
```
  2,190
+ 2,998
```

9
```
  23,988
+    656
```

10
```
  23,510
+  5,666
```

Name: _____ Date: _____

Take It Away: Subtraction Practice

To find the difference in a subtraction equation, use what you know about place value to solve the problem.

Place value can be shown like this:

Number	Tens	Ones
78	7	8
54	5	4
24	2	4

Sometimes you have to regroup your numbers.

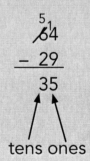

Directions: Solve the problems.

1
```
  4,588
−   302
```

2
```
  1,087
−   347
```

3
```
    585
−   569
```

4
```
  5,983
−   499
```

5
```
  4,990
−    37
```

6
```
  3,856
− 1,856
```

7
```
    784
−   692
```

8
```
  5,381
−   371
```

9
```
  9,344
− 4,900
```

Name:_____ Date: _____

Follow That Symbol!

Directions: Solve the problems.

1 $54.29
    + $16.39

2   34,990
    − 12,323

3   33,000
    + 4,599

4   51,009
    − 11,932

5 $122.58
    + $3.41

6   229
    + 45

7   7,782
    + 354

8   92,990
    − 4,588

9 $34.25
    + $12.77

10   43,099
    + 4,665

11 $121.45
    − $54.69

12   87,344
    − 52,770

13   122,330
    − 14,566

14   445
    + 661

15   772,544
    + 45,877

Name:_____ Date: _____

Place Value and Word Problems

Directions: Solve the word problems.

1 Hank Aaron hit 755 career home runs, Babe Ruth hit 714 home runs, Willie Mays hit 660 home runs, and Frank Robinson hit 586 home runs. How many home runs did they hit altogether?

2 A striped skunk is 800 millimeters long from the tip of its nose to the tip of its tail. A spotted skunk is 563 millimeters long. How much longer is the striped skunk?

Name:_____ Date: _____

More Practice with Place Value

Directions: Solve the word problems.

1 In my school, there are 92 kindergarteners, 87 first graders, and 82 second graders. How many students in my school are in grades K–2?

2 The weights of four raccoons were 12 pounds, 48 pounds, 32 pounds, and 25 pounds. How much did they weigh altogether?

Name:_____ Date: _____

Finding Your Own Place

Directions: Write an addition problem and a subtraction word problem. Then, switch papers with a partner and solve the problems.

1 _____

_____

_____

2 _____

_____

_____

Name: _____ Date: _____

Getting to the Bottom of Multiplication

Multiplication means adding a number to itself a particular number of times.

$3 \times 4 = 12.$ This means to add 3 four times: $3 + 3 + 3 + 3 = 12.$

With larger numbers, there are steps to take to find the correct number.

$$\begin{array}{r} 45 \\ \times\ 25 \\ \hline 225 \\ 900 \\ \hline 1{,}125 \end{array}$$

- Multiply the ones.
- Multiply the tens.
- Add the partial products.

Directions: Solve the multiplication problems.

❶
$$\begin{array}{r} 79 \\ \times\ 31 \\ \hline \end{array}$$

❷
$$\begin{array}{r} 54 \\ \times\ 18 \\ \hline \end{array}$$

❸
$$\begin{array}{r} 88 \\ \times\ 21 \\ \hline \end{array}$$

❹
$$\begin{array}{r} 65 \\ \times\ 29 \\ \hline \end{array}$$

❺
$$\begin{array}{r} 57 \\ \times\ 21 \\ \hline \end{array}$$

❻
$$\begin{array}{r} 61 \\ \times\ 20 \\ \hline \end{array}$$

❼
$$\begin{array}{r} 34 \\ \times\ 30 \\ \hline \end{array}$$

❽
$$\begin{array}{r} 81 \\ \times\ 28 \\ \hline \end{array}$$

❾
$$\begin{array}{r} 54 \\ \times\ 28 \\ \hline \end{array}$$

Name: _____ Date: _____

Multiplying Multiple Digits

Directions: Solve the problems.

❶
$$\begin{array}{r} 369 \\ \times\ \ 5 \\ \hline \end{array}$$

❷
$$\begin{array}{r} 428 \\ \times\ \ 3 \\ \hline \end{array}$$

❸
$$\begin{array}{r} 123 \\ \times\ \ 6 \\ \hline \end{array}$$

❹
$$\begin{array}{r} 430 \\ \times\ \ 2 \\ \hline \end{array}$$

❺
$$\begin{array}{r} 923 \\ \times\ \ 8 \\ \hline \end{array}$$

❻
$$\begin{array}{r} 745 \\ \times\ \ 2 \\ \hline \end{array}$$

❼
$$\begin{array}{r} 598 \\ \times\ \ 4 \\ \hline \end{array}$$

❽
$$\begin{array}{r} 649 \\ \times\ \ 6 \\ \hline \end{array}$$

❾
$$\begin{array}{r} 281 \\ \times\ \ 6 \\ \hline \end{array}$$

❿
$$\begin{array}{r} 510 \\ \times\ \ 3 \\ \hline \end{array}$$

Name:_____ Date: _____

Practicing Math with Equivalent Measurements

1 minute = 60 seconds

1 hour = 60 minutes

1 day = 24 hours

1 year = 365 days

Directions: Read the word problems. For each problem, write a number sentence and solve it. Use the above equivalent measurements to find your answers.

1 How many days are in 6 years, excluding leap years?	**2** How many seconds are in 1 hour?
3 How many seconds are in 1 day?	**4** How many minutes are in 42 hours?

Name: _____ Date: _____

Multiplication Body Facts

1 minute = 60 seconds

1 hour = 60 minutes

1 day = 24 hours

1 year = 365 days

Directions: Read the word problems. For each problem, write a number sentence and solve it. Use the above equivalent measurements to find your answers.

1 A child's heart beats about 90 times a minute. How many times does it beat in 1 hour?	**2** The heart pumps about 4 quarts of blood each minute. How many quarts of blood does it pump in 1 day?
3 On average, a person blinks approximately 960 times in an hour. How many times will a person blink in 16 hours?	**4** On average, a person sneezes about 3 times a day. In the month of January, how many times will a person sneeze?

Name:_____ Date: _____

Multiply for Answers

Directions: Read the word problems. For each problem, write a number sentence and solve it.

---

1 A queen termite can lay 25 eggs a minute. How many eggs can she lay in 60 minutes?

2 A cheese factory makes 72 boxes of cheese every day. How many boxes will they make in 4 days?

---

3 Mr. Kramer passes out packages of markers to his 28 students. Each package has 24 markers. How many markers are there in all?

4 The jewelry store has 150 necklaces on a display table. There are 6 tables. How many necklaces are on display in all?

---

5 A roller skate has 4 wheels. If 52 kids are roller skating and they each are wearing two skates, how many wheels are there in all?

6 The librarian checked in 42 books from one classroom. If all 22 classes brought in the same amount, how many books will the librarian check in?

Name: _____ Date: _____

What's the Missing Factor?

Directions: Find the missing factors.

1 9 × _____ = 1,935	**2** 17 × _____ = 833
3 2 × _____ = 1,216	**4** 6 × _____ = 3,084
5 3 × _____ = 2,124	**6** 55 × _____ = 1,100
7 7 × _____ = 2,940	**8** 37 × _____ = 1,369
9 7 × _____ = 6,720	**10** 22 × _____ = 1,254

Name:_____ Date: _____

Finding Both Missing Factors

Directions: Find the missing numbers for the number sentences below. Then, tell what strategies you used. *Note:* There is more than one correct solution.

1 _____ _____ _____ × _____ = 1,884

Show your work.

What strategy did you use to find the solution? _____

_____

_____

2 _____ _____ _____ × _____ = 3,492

Show your work.

What strategy did you use to find the solution? _____

_____

_____

3 _____ _____ _____ × _____ = 1,575

Show your work.

What strategy did you use to find the solution? _____

_____

_____

Name:_____ Date: _____

Dividing It Up

> **Division** is a quick and easy way to subtract the same number several times.
>
> $$27 \div 9 = 3$$
>
> This is the same as subtracting 9 from 27 three times.
>
> $$27 - 9 - 9 - 9 = 3$$

Directions: Solve the problems.

1 $8\overline{)64}$ **2** $9\overline{)99}$ **3** $6\overline{)126}$

4 $4\overline{)92}$ **5** $7\overline{)749}$ **6** $3\overline{)201}$

7 $6\overline{)312}$ **8** $8\overline{)120}$ **9** $5\overline{)85}$

Name: _____ Date: _____

What's Remaining?

Some division problems divide evenly and other times you are left with a **remainder**.

$$27 \div 9 = 3$$

But, what happens when you divide 29 by 9?

It divides evenly 3 times, but that is only 27. Therefore, there are 2 left over.

This solution has a remainder of 2. It can be written 3 R2.

Directions: Solve the problems. The answers may or may not have remainders.

1 $8\overline{)84}$ **2** $9\overline{)39}$ **3** $6\overline{)96}$

4 $4\overline{)87}$ **5** $7\overline{)102}$ **6** $3\overline{)22}$

7 $6\overline{)648}$ **8** $8\overline{)113}$ **9** $5\overline{)125}$

Name:_____ Date: _____

Multiplication and Division Connection

Division and multiplication are opposite math operations. Multiplication can be used to check division.

$36 \div 4 = 9 \qquad 9 \times 4 = 36$

$63 \div 8 = 7 \text{ R7} \qquad 8 \times 7 = 56 + 7 = 63$

Directions: Solve the following division problems. Then, use multiplication to check your answers.

1 $8\overline{)82}$

2 $9\overline{)78}$

3 $8\overline{)899}$

4 $6\overline{)124}$

5 $3\overline{)591}$

6 $8\overline{)673}$

Name:_____ Date: _____

Mystery Division Problems

Directions: Find the value of x.

1 180 ÷ x = 60

2 45 ÷ x = 3

3 68 ÷ x = 4

4 22 ÷ x = 2

5 88 ÷ x = 11

6 90 ÷ x = 6

7 144 ÷ x = 12

8 225 ÷ x = 9

Name: _____ Date: _____

Solving Division Word Problems

Directions: Solve the word problems.

1 Mrs. Walker bought a large box of popsicles for the fourth graders to eat on a hot day. The box had 134 popsicles. It was divided among 5 classes. If each class received the same number of popsicles, how many popsicles did each class receive?

Were there any popsicles remaining? _____

If so, how many? _____

3 An artist needs to buy 47 paintbrushes of all sizes. If paintbrushes come in packages of 5, how many packages should the artist buy?

Were there any paintbrushes remaining? _____

If so, how many? _____

2 Josephine has $134.00 to buy candles for a wedding. If the candles cost $6.00, how many candles can she buy?

Did she have any money left over? _____

If so, how much? _____

4 The restaurant supplier needs to purchase 580 rolls of paper towels. Each package comes with 9 paper towel rolls. How many packages should the supplier purchase?

Were there any paper towel rolls remaining? _____

If so, how many? _____

Name:_____ Date: _____

Half Is Half

Equivalent fractions have the same value.

$$\frac{1}{2} = \frac{2}{4} = \frac{4}{8}$$

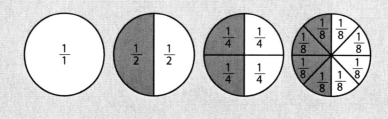

Directions: Show how these fractions are the same using numbers and pictures.

1 $\frac{1}{3} = \frac{2}{6} = \frac{3}{9}$

2 $\frac{1}{4} = \frac{2}{8} = \frac{3}{12}$

Name: _____ Date: _____

Making Things Equal

....

Equivalent fractions have the same value.

$$\frac{1}{2} = \frac{2}{4}$$

Directions: Solve each problem below by finding equivalent fractions.

1 $\frac{2}{5} = \frac{x}{10}$

$x =$ __4__

2 $\frac{1}{3} = \frac{x}{6}$

$x =$ ____

3 $\frac{x}{4} = \frac{6}{8}$

$x =$ ____

4 $\frac{x}{8} = \frac{1}{4}$

$x =$ ____

Name:_____ Date: _____

Making Equivalent Fractions

To make equivalent fractions, multiply the numerator and denominator by the same number.

$$\frac{1 \times 2}{5 \times 2} = \frac{2}{10} \qquad \frac{1 \times 3}{5 \times 3} = \frac{3}{15}$$

Multiplying the numerator and denominator by the same number is the same as multiplying by 1.

Directions: Look at each fraction below. Write two fractions that are equivalent in value.

1 $\frac{2}{3}$ = _____ = _____

2 $\frac{3}{8}$ = _____ = _____

3 $\frac{4}{5}$ = _____ = _____

4 $\frac{9}{10}$ = _____ = _____

5 $\frac{8}{13}$ = _____ = _____

Name: _____ Date: _____

More or Less? Comparing Fractions

Compare the following fractions. Which fraction is greater?

$\frac{1}{2}$ or $\frac{1}{3}$

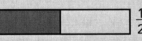

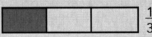

$\frac{1}{2}$ is bigger than $\frac{1}{3}$

Directions: Determine which fraction is greater. Show your work in each box.

❶ $\frac{2}{7}$ and $\frac{4}{5}$

The greater fraction = _____

❷ $\frac{7}{16}$ and $\frac{3}{22}$

The greater fraction = _____

Name:_____ Date: _____

Fraction Evaluation: Measuring Value

Directions: Compare the fractions below. Use the <, >, and = to fill in the circles.
You can also use fraction bars to help you solve the problems.

1 $\frac{4}{5}$ ◯ $\frac{7}{8}$

5 $\frac{9}{18}$ ◯ $\frac{6}{12}$

2 $\frac{1}{6}$ ◯ $\frac{3}{8}$

6 $\frac{6}{15}$ ◯ $\frac{5}{16}$

3 $\frac{5}{12}$ ◯ $\frac{7}{10}$

7 $\frac{25}{250}$ ◯ $\frac{2}{10}$

4 $\frac{1}{4}$ ◯ $\frac{2}{8}$

8 $\frac{8}{24}$ ◯ $\frac{6}{8}$

Name: _____ Date: _____

Writing Fraction Word Problems

Directions: Read the word problem below and solve it. Then, write your own word problem and trade with someone to solve.

1 Stella loves fresh berry pie. This summer, her mom made her a pie to share with her dad. She ate $\frac{1}{8}$ of a pie and her dad ate $\frac{1}{4}$ of a pie. Who ate more? Show your work.

Solution:

2 Word problem:

_____

_____

_____

Solution:

Name: _____ Date: _____

Adding and Subtracting Pieces of the Pie

Imagine that a pie is cut into 8 equal slices. Joe ate 3 slices. Sara ate 2 slices. Add the numerators and the denominator stays the same.

$$\frac{3}{8} + \frac{2}{8} = \frac{5}{8}$$

Directions: Draw a picture to solve each picture. Write your answer on the line.

1 $\frac{2}{5} + \frac{1}{5} =$ _____

2 $\frac{4}{6} + \frac{1}{6} =$ _____

3 $\frac{3}{8} + \frac{3}{8} =$ _____

4 $\frac{6}{12} + \frac{4}{12} =$ _____

5 $\frac{7}{14} - \frac{2}{14} =$ _____

6 $\frac{7}{7} - \frac{3}{7} =$ _____

Name: _____ Date: _____

More Than a Whole

A whole number is sometimes involved when adding or subtracting fractions. **Mixed numbers** are numbers that include both a whole number and a fraction, such as $1\frac{3}{5}$. You can add and subtract mixed numbers just like fractions.

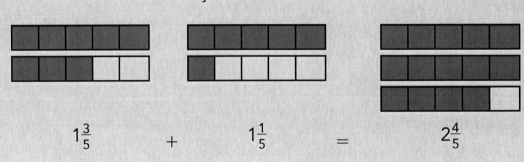

$$1\frac{3}{5} \qquad + \qquad 1\frac{1}{5} \qquad = \qquad 2\frac{4}{5}$$

Directions: Solve the mixed numbers by adding or subtracting. Draw a picture to show your work.

1 $6\frac{6}{8} - 1\frac{1}{8} =$

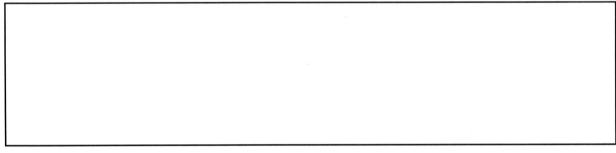

2 $12\frac{3}{5} - 6\frac{2}{5} =$

Name: _____ Date: _____

Breaking Apart A Fraction

You can represent a fraction by creating a sum of fractions with a common denominator.

$$\frac{4}{6} = \frac{1}{6} + \frac{1}{6} + \frac{1}{6} + \frac{1}{6}$$

$$\frac{4}{6} = \frac{3}{6} + \frac{1}{6}$$

$$\frac{4}{6} = \frac{2}{6} + \frac{2}{6}$$

Directions: Look at each fraction below. Break apart the fraction by writing a sum of smaller fractions with a common denominator.

1 $\frac{6}{8}$

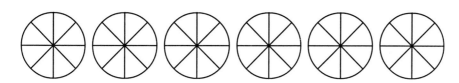

_____

2 $\frac{7}{10}$

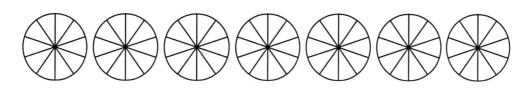

_____

3 $\frac{4}{12}$

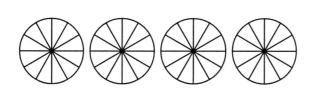

_____

Name:_____ Date: _____

Add Them Up!

Directions: Add the smaller fractions and whole numbers.

❶ $1 + 1 + \frac{1}{8} + \frac{1}{8} =$ _____

❷ $\frac{1}{7} + \frac{1}{7} + \frac{1}{7} + \frac{1}{7} + \frac{1}{7} + \frac{1}{7} =$ _____

❸ $5 + 6 + \frac{1}{6} + \frac{1}{6} =$ _____

❹ $\frac{1}{12} + \frac{1}{12} + \frac{1}{12} + \frac{1}{12} + \frac{1}{12} =$ _____

❺ $\frac{2}{7} + \frac{2}{7} =$ _____

❻ $10 + 10 + \frac{1}{3} + \frac{1}{3} =$ _____

❼ $\frac{1}{5} + \frac{1}{5} + \frac{1}{5} + \frac{1}{5} =$ _____

❽ $4 + 4 + \frac{1}{4} =$ _____

❾ $\frac{2}{8} + \frac{2}{8} + \frac{2}{8} =$ _____

❿ $\frac{3}{9} + \frac{3}{9} =$ _____

Name:_____ Date: _____

Mixing It Up with Mixed Numbers

Adding **mixed numbers** is easier when you know how to change a mixed number into an improper fraction or change an improper fraction into a mixed number.

$$1\frac{2}{6} + \frac{5}{6} = 1\frac{7}{6}$$

If you get an improper fraction, change it to a mixed number by dividing.

$$
\begin{array}{r}
1\frac{1}{6} \\
6\overline{)\,7} \\
-6 \\
\hline
1
\end{array}
$$

Add the whole number and the mixed number together.

$$1\frac{2}{6} + \frac{5}{6} = 1\frac{7}{6}$$

Directions: Add these mixed numbers together by changing the mixed numbers into fractions. Show your work in the box.

1 $2\frac{2}{3} + 3\frac{2}{3} =$ _____

2 $6\frac{3}{8} + 2\frac{7}{8} =$ _____

Name:_____ Date: _____

Adding Subtraction to the Mix

Subtracting **mixed numbers** is easier when you know how to change a mixed number into an improper fraction or change an improper fraction into a mixed number.

$$2\frac{1}{5} - 1\frac{4}{5} = ?$$

$$2\frac{1}{5} = \frac{5}{5} + \frac{5}{5} + \frac{1}{5} = \frac{11}{5} \qquad \text{and} \qquad 1\frac{4}{5} = \frac{5}{5} + \frac{4}{5} = \frac{9}{5}$$

$$\frac{11}{5} - \frac{9}{5} = \frac{2}{5} \quad \text{so} \quad 2\frac{1}{5} - 1\frac{4}{5} = \frac{2}{5}$$

Directions: Subtract these mixed numbers by changing the mixed numbers into improper fractions.

1 $8\frac{1}{6} - 3\frac{4}{6} =$ _____

2 $7\frac{5}{12} - 4\frac{7}{12} =$ _____

3 $12\frac{2}{7} - 6\frac{5}{7} =$ _____

Name:_____ Date: _____

Adding Mixed Numbers and Whole Numbers

Directions: Solve the problems. Show your work in the box.

1 $3\frac{2}{5} + 6 =$

2 $2\frac{1}{2} + 8 =$

3 $6\frac{3}{4} + 12 =$

Name:_____ Date: _____

Breaking Bread: Solving Fraction Word Problems

Directions: Solve the problems by writing a number sentence and drawing a picture that fits the story. Show your work in the box.

1 Liz went to the bakery to buy muffins to share with her friends. She bought a dozen muffins. 4 were blueberry, 5 were banana nut, and the rest were pumpkin muffins. How many pumpkin muffins did Liz buy?

2 Michael wanted to share bagels with his friends for breakfast. He chose to buy 10 bagels. There were 2 poppy seed, 3 cinnamon raisin, and 2 plain bagels. The rest were wheat bagels. How many wheat bagels did Michael buy?

Name:_____ Date: _____

Fraction Solutions

An **improper fraction** has a numerator that is greater than (or equal to) the denominator.

$\frac{3}{2}$, $\frac{6}{3}$, and $\frac{9}{2}$ are all improper fractions.

$\frac{3}{2}$ is an improper fraction that can also be thought of as "three halves."

$\frac{3}{2} = 3 \times \frac{1}{2}$

Directions: Look at the improper fractions below. Write each improper fraction as a multiplication sentence and as words. Draw a picture to show the amount.

 $\frac{6}{4}$ _____ × _____

_____

 $\frac{8}{5}$ _____ × _____

_____

Name:_____ Date: _____

Improper Multiplication and Addition

Multiplying whole numbers is repeated addition.

$$5 \times 3 = 5 + 5 + 5 = 15$$

Improper fractions also equal a repeated addition sentence.

$$\frac{7}{3} = \frac{1}{3} + \frac{1}{3} + \frac{1}{3} + \frac{1}{3} + \frac{1}{3} + \frac{1}{3} + \frac{1}{3} = 7 \times \frac{1}{3}$$

Directions: Write the following improper fractions as an addition number sentence and a multiplication number sentence. The first one has been done for you.

	Improper fraction	Multiplication sentence	Addition sentence
1	$\frac{8}{3}$	$8 \times \frac{1}{3}$	$\frac{1}{3} + \frac{1}{3} + \frac{1}{3} + \frac{1}{3} + \frac{1}{3} + \frac{1}{3} + \frac{1}{3} + \frac{1}{3}$
2	$\frac{9}{4}$		
3	$\frac{7}{2}$		
4	$\frac{5}{2}$		
5	$\frac{12}{5}$		
6	$\frac{10}{3}$		
7	$\frac{6}{2}$		

Name:_____ Date: _____

Fraction Word Problems

Directions: Read the word problems. Show your work in the box.

1 Nola invited 15 friends to her birthday party. The girls ate pizza for dinner. They ate $\frac{2}{4}$ of the pepperoni pizza and $\frac{1}{4}$ of the cheese pizza. How much pizza did they eat altogether?

2 On Monday, Sergio made $\frac{3}{10}$ of his shots in the basketball game. On Tuesday, he made $\frac{1}{10}$ of his shots in the basketball game. How many shots did he make altogether?

3 The cook needed to hard-boil some eggs. She used $\frac{1}{2}$ a dozen eggs for breakfast and $\frac{3}{4}$ of a dozen eggs for lunch. How many eggs did she use altogether?

Name:_____ Date: _____

Keeping the Order: Multiplying Fractions

When multiplying fractions by whole numbers, follow the same rules used to multiply two fractions.

The whole number is considered a fraction with a denominator of 1. After multiplying, turn the improper fraction back into a mixed number.

$$8 \times \frac{4}{5}$$

$$\frac{8}{1} \times \frac{4}{5} = \frac{32}{5}$$

$$\frac{32}{5} = 6\frac{2}{5}$$

Directions: Solve the problems below by multiplying the whole numbers by fractions. Show your work.

1 $6 \times \frac{1}{2} =$

2 $18 \times \frac{2}{3} =$

3 $10 \times \frac{3}{5} =$

Name:_____ Date: _____

A Fraction of a Whole Number

Directions: Solve the problems below by multiplying the whole numbers by fractions. Show your work.

1 $5 \times \frac{3}{9} =$

2 $11 \times \frac{4}{11} =$

3 $7 \times \frac{6}{8} =$

4 $12 \times \frac{1}{4} =$

Name:_____ Date: _____

Real World Fractions

Directions: Read the word problems. Solve the problems by multiplying the whole numbers by fractions. Show your work.

❶ Chloe has 12 pencils. If $\frac{3}{4}$ of them are broken, how many pencils are broken? _____

❷ Mr. Garcia baked 24 cupcakes. He will bring $\frac{1}{3}$ of them to a party. How many cupcakes will he bring to the party? _____

❸ The soccer players kicked 18 soccer balls to the goal. If $\frac{2}{3}$ of the balls made it in the goal, how many soccer balls did not make it in the goal? _____

Name:_____ Date: _____

Fraction Party Riddles

Directions: Read the word problems. Solve the problems by multiplying the whole numbers by fractions. Show your work.

1 The Niles family is having a barbecue. They are inviting over family and friends. If they want to grill $\frac{2}{3}$ pound of ribs for each person and 15 people are eating ribs, how many ribs do they need to grill?

2 Some people at the Niles family party will be eating salmon. If the Niles family wants to cook $\frac{3}{5}$ pound of salmon for each person and 12 people are eating salmon, how much salmon do they need to cook?

3 The Niles family definitely wants everyone to eat dessert, too. If they estimate that each guest will have about $\frac{1}{6}$ of a pie, how many pies do they need to serve 24 guests?

Name:_____ Date: _____

More Fraction Riddles

Directions: Read the word problems. Solve the problems by multiplying the whole numbers by fractions. Show your work.

1 Mr. Thomas wants to make sure his students have enough crayons. If each student needs about $\frac{6}{15}$ of a package and he has 26 students, how many packages does the class need?

2 The cafeteria helpers cut the fruit into pieces each morning. Fruit cups have 12 pieces in them. If 18 students eat $\frac{9}{12}$ of the fruit cup, how much fruit do they need?

3 The principal is observing how much garbage each class recycles. 20 classrooms each fill $\frac{2}{3}$ of a bag. How much garbage did they recycle altogether?

Name: _____ Date: _____

Fractions with Tens and Hundreds

When a fraction has 10 as the denominator, you can easily find an equivalent fraction with 100 as a denominator.

$$\frac{3}{10} = \frac{30}{100}$$

Remember that both the numerator and the denominator are multiplied by 10.

Directions: Find the missing numerators and write them on the spaces provided.

1 $\frac{4}{10} = \frac{x}{100}$ x = _____	**2** $\frac{1}{10} = \frac{x}{100}$ x = _____
3 $\frac{7}{10} = \frac{x}{100}$ x = _____	**4** $\frac{5}{10} = \frac{x}{100}$ x = _____

When you add two fractions, they must have the same denominator.

$$\frac{3}{10} + \frac{3}{10} = \frac{6}{10}$$

$$\frac{7}{10} + \frac{7}{10} = \frac{14}{10} = 1\frac{4}{10}$$

Directions: Add the fractions below.

5 $\frac{4}{10} + \frac{6}{10} =$ _____	**6** $\frac{2}{10} + \frac{9}{10} =$ _____
7 $\frac{4}{10} + \frac{7}{10} =$ _____	**8** $\frac{8}{10} + \frac{6}{10} =$ _____

Name:_____ Date: _____

Putting Tens and Hundreds Together

How do you add the following fractions?

$$\frac{3}{10} + \frac{5}{100}$$

We know that the denominators need to be equal to add fractions. This means you have to find an equivalent fraction of $\frac{3}{10}$.

$$\frac{3}{10} = \frac{30}{100}$$

$$\frac{30}{100} + \frac{5}{100} = \frac{35}{100}$$

Directions: Solve the problems below. Show how to find equivalent fractions before you add.

1 $\frac{6}{10} + \frac{16}{100}$

2 $\frac{1}{10} + \frac{25}{100}$

3 $\frac{4}{10} + \frac{42}{100}$

4 $\frac{7}{10} + \frac{11}{100}$

Name:_____ Date: _____

Turning a Decimal Into a Fraction

A **decimal** is a fraction whose denominator is a power of ten (10, 100, 1000, and so on) and whose numerator is shown to the right of a decimal point. A decimal, like a fraction, is not a whole number. It is *part* of a number.

$$\frac{4}{10} = 0.4 \qquad \text{four tenths}$$

$$\frac{4}{100} = 0.04 \qquad \text{four hundredths}$$

$$\frac{4}{1,000} = 0.004 \qquad \text{four thousandths}$$

Directions: Change the fractions into decimals.

1 $\frac{5}{10}$ _____	**2** $\frac{9}{10}$ _____
3 $\frac{2}{10}$ _____	**4** $\frac{7}{100}$ _____
5 $\frac{4}{100}$ _____	**6** $\frac{26}{100}$ _____
7 $\frac{80}{1,000}$ _____	**8** $\frac{4}{10}$ _____
9 $\frac{6}{100}$ _____	**10** $\frac{98}{100}$ _____
11 $\frac{590}{1,000}$ _____	**12** $\frac{1}{10}$ _____
13 $\frac{55}{100}$ _____	**14** $\frac{802}{1,000}$ _____

Name: _____ Date: _____

Getting Decimals in Line

Directions: Change each group of fractions into decimals. Then, place the decimals in order from greatest to least.

1 $\dfrac{5}{10}$ $\dfrac{9}{100}$ $\dfrac{6}{100}$ $\dfrac{7}{100}$ $\dfrac{25}{100}$

_____ _____ _____ _____ _____

2 $\dfrac{9}{10}$ $\dfrac{6}{100}$ $\dfrac{4}{100}$ $\dfrac{61}{1,000}$ $\dfrac{6}{10}$

_____ _____ _____ _____ _____

3 $\dfrac{4}{10}$ $\dfrac{12}{100}$ $\dfrac{8}{10}$ $\dfrac{2}{1,000}$ $\dfrac{57}{100}$

_____ _____ _____ _____ _____

4 $\dfrac{9}{10}$ $\dfrac{6}{1,000}$ $\dfrac{9}{100}$ $\dfrac{57}{100}$ $\dfrac{2}{100}$

_____ _____ _____ _____ _____

Directions: Mark the letter of each value in the correct location on the number line.

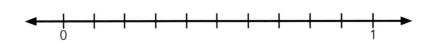

0   1

5 a 0.75

6 b 0.29

7 c 0.15

8 d 0.50

Name:_____ Date: _____

Decimals Large and Small

Directions: Look at the decimals. Use the <, >, and = signs to show how the values compare.

1 0.44 _____ 0.4

6 0.72 _____ 0.27

2 0.75 _____ 0.55

7 0.11 _____ 0.10

3 0.62 _____ 0.52

8 0.30 _____ 0.3

4 0.80 _____ 0.8

9 0.94 _____ 0.99

5 0.99 _____ 0.9

10 0.10 _____ 0.01

Name: _____ Date: _____

Measure It Up!

Directions: Use a ruler with centimeters and inches to measure the following items:

1 The length of a pencil is _____ inches _____ centimeters

2 The length of a paper clip is _____ inches _____ centimeters

3 The length of a string is _____ inches _____ centimeters

4 The length of a marker is _____ inches _____ centimeters

5 The length of a button is _____ inches _____ centimeters

6 The length of a crayon is _____ inches _____ centimeters

> We also use measurement to weigh items. Items can be weighed in pounds, ounces, grams, and centigrams.

Directions: Circle the best unit of measurement for each object.

7 a button on a jacket

    a. centigrams   **b.** grams

8 a puppy

    a. pounds   **b.** ounces

9 a paperclip

    a. pounds   **b.** centigrams

10 a brick

    a. ounces   **b.** pounds

Name:_____ Date: _____

Relative Sizes of Measurement

Directions: Circle the correct answer.

1 What unit would you use to measure the length of a swimming pool?

      inches   miles   meters

2 What unit would you use to measure the weight of a blue whale?

      ounces   pounds   tons

3 What unit would you use to measure the time it takes to watch a movie?

      seconds   hours   days

4 What unit would you use to measure the amount of liquid in a baby bottle?

      fluid ounces   quarts   gallons

5 What unit would you use to measure the time it takes to walk to school?

      minutes   days   seconds

6 What unit would you use to measure the weight of a basketball?

      ounces   pounds   tons

7 What unit would you use to measure the length of a pencil?

      centimeters   miles   yards

Name:_____ Date: _____

Equivalent Measurements

Units of measurement have equivalent values. Here are some other measurement equivalents:

Length

12 inches = 1 foot

10 millimeters = 1 centimeter

1 meter = 100 centimeters

1 kilometer = 1,000 meters

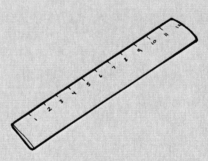

Weight

16 ounces = 1 pound

2,000 pounds = 1 ton

Liquid Measurements

8 fluid ounces = 1 cup

2 cups = 1 pint

2 pints = 1 quart

4 quarts = 1 gallon

Time

60 seconds = 1 minute

60 minutes = 1 hour

24 hours = 1 day

Equivalent Measurements *(cont.)*

Directions: Use the measurement equivalents to complete the tables below.

1

Inches	Feet
24 in.	
48 in.	
120 in.	
	3 ft.

2

Centimeters	Meters
400 cm	
660 cm	
	24 m
	8 m

3

Ounces	Pounds
32 oz.	
160 oz.	
96 oz.	
	4 lb.

4

Pounds	Tons
8,000 lb.	
14,000 lb.	
	12 tons
	20 tons

5

Pints	Quarts
8 pints	
40 pints	
	800 quarts
	450 quarts

6

Cups	Pints
26 cups	
88 cups	
	40 pints
	200 pints

7

Minutes	Hours
120 min.	
240 min.	
2,400 min.	
	8 hrs.

8

Seconds	Minutes
120 sec.	
1,200 sec.	
	40 min.
	60 min.

Name:_____ Date: _____

Solving Word Problems

Directions: Write an equation and solution on the lines provided.

1 At the toy store, jacks cost $1.59 a set. How much would it cost to buy 20 sets?

_____

2 To beat the heat, a group of 7 neighbors bought a big plastic pool. It cost $64.98. How much did each neighbor pay?

_____

3 Jose bought a bike that cost $120.80. Alec bought a bike that cost $219.88. How much less did Jose pay than Alec?

_____

4 A red wolf has a tail that is 42 centimeters long. A grey wolf has a tail 50 centimeters long. How much longer is the grey wolf's tail?

_____

5 Parker needs a rope that is $2\frac{1}{2}$ feet long for an art project. How many inches is the rope?

_____

6 Ella wants to cut her hair. She asked her hair dresser to cut off 9 centimeters. How many millimeters did she ask to cut?

_____

Name:_____ Date: _____

Tick Tock Goes the Clock:
Elapsed Time Problems

Directions: Solve the word problems.

1 Evan has to be at school at 8:30 A.M. The bell to go home rings at 2:30 P.M. How long is his school day in hours?

_____

2 Jenna's soccer game starts at 4:00 P.M. She plays for an hour and then goes home. She goes to bed 3 hours later. What time does she go to bed?

_____

3 Joaquin has to be up by 6:00 A.M. He really wants to get 10 hours of sleep. What time should he go to sleep?

_____

4 Betsy catches the bus at 7:15 A.M. It is an hour and a half bus ride to school. What time does she arrive at school?

_____

5 Felicia's birthday party starts at 11:30 A.M. Her friends stay until 2:15 P.M. How long did her party last?

_____

6 The train is scheduled to leave the station at 5:04 P.M. It is delayed by 20 minutes. Then it makes its first stop at 6:20 P.M. How long was the first part of the trip?

_____

Name: _____ Date: _____

Finding Perimeter: Distance Around a Space

Perimeter is the distance around the edges of an object. The perimeter of a rectangle is found by adding all four sides or by adding the length and width and multiplying by 2.

$$P = l + l + w + w$$

$$P = 2(l + w)$$

Directions: Find the perimeter of the rectangles.

❶

20 ft.

10 ft.

P = _____

❷

8 yd.

3 yd.

P = _____

❸

7 in.

4 in.

P = _____

❹

110 ft.

30 ft.

P = _____

Finding Perimeter: Distance Around a Space *(cont.)*

Directions: Draw the shapes of the dimensions described. Then, find the perimeter of the rectangles.

5 What is the perimeter of a bedroom that is 25 feet long and 12 feet wide?

_____

6 What is the perimeter of a room that is 45 meters long and 40 meters wide?

_____

7 What is the perimeter of a building that is 70 meters long and 20 meters wide?

_____

8 What is the perimeter of a cafeteria that is 60 feet long and 50 feet wide?

_____

Name: _____ Date: _____

How Large Is Your Area?

Area is the amount of surface that a two-dimensional shape covers. The area of a rectangle is found by multiplying the length by the width.

$$A = l \times w$$

The answer is always given in **square units**.

Directions: Find the area of the rectangles. *Hint:* The answer will be in square units.

❶

6 in.

3 in.

A = _____

❷

7 ft.

5 ft.

A = _____

❸

80 m

50 m

A = _____

❹

50 cm

50 cm

A = _____

How Large Is Your Area? *(cont.)*

. . . .

Directions: Find the area of the rectangles in these word problems. Draw and label the unit of measurement in your answer. *Hint*: The answer will be in square units.

5 What is the area of a table 6 feet long and 5 feet wide?

_____

6 What is the area of a paper 28 centimeters long and 22 centimeters wide?

_____

Name:_____ Date: _____

Line Them Up: Making Line Plots

A **line plot** shows data on a number line with various symbols to show frequency, such as an x. An x is marked each time the same measurement appears. A line plot makes it easy to see which measurements appear the most or least.

Directions: Use the data below to make a line plot below. Then, answer the questions.

Length of erasers							
$3\frac{1}{2}$ inches	||	$2\frac{3}{4}$ inches	||	$1\frac{3}{4}$ inches	|||	1 inch	|
$3\frac{1}{4}$ inches	|	$2\frac{1}{2}$ inches	|||	$1\frac{1}{4}$ inches	||	2 inches	||

❶ Plot the data on this line plot. Make sure to give the line plot a title and label the axis.

_____

1 in.　　$1\frac{1}{4}$ in.　　$1\frac{3}{4}$ in.　　2 in.　　$2\frac{1}{2}$ in.　　$2\frac{3}{4}$ in.　　$3\frac{1}{4}$ in.　　$3\frac{1}{2}$ in.

❷ What is the most common length of eraser? _____

❸ What is the longest eraser? _____

❹ What is the shortest eraser? _____

❺ What is the difference between the longest and shortest erasers?

_____

❻ Write one question that can be answered by using the line plot.

_____

_____

Name:_____ Date: _____

Connecting the Dots: Interpreting Data on a Line Plot

Directions: Use the line plot to answer the questions.

Length of Books Checked Out From School Library

X						
X			X			
X		X	X	X		
X	X	X	X	X		
X	X	X	X	X		X
X	X	X	X	X	X	X
$6\frac{1}{2}$ in.	7 in.	$7\frac{1}{2}$ in.	8 in.	$8\frac{1}{2}$ in.	9 in.	$9\frac{1}{2}$ in.

1 Which size book was the most popular? _____

2 Which size book was the least popular? _____

3 What is the difference in length between the longest and shortest books?

_____

Name: _____ Date: _____

Circle Round: Measuring Angles

A **circle** is a set of points, all of which are the same distance from a center point. There are 360 degrees in a circle.

An **angle** is the space between two diverging lines. Angles have a **vertex** (point) and two sides (**rays**). Angles are measured in degrees.

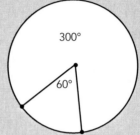

Directions: Find the measurement of the missing angles.

1

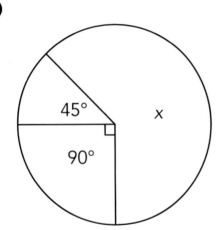

2

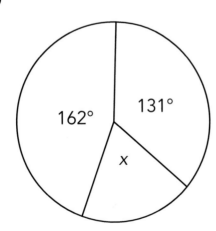

Name:_____ Date: _____

Cutting Through the Circle

Directions: Use a protractor to draw the angles in each circle below. Label each angle.

1 Draw and label angles measuring 180°, 60°, and 120°.

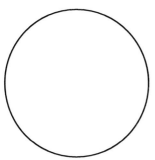

2 Draw and label angles measuring 270°, 30°, and 60°.

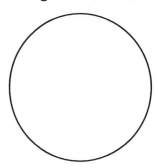

3 Draw and label angles measuring 95°, 75°, and 190°.

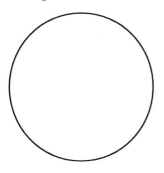

4 Draw and label angles measuring 45°, 85°, and 230°.

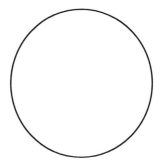

5 Draw and label angles measuring 120°, 120°, and 120°.

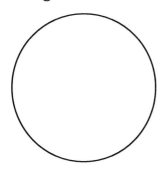

6 Draw and label angles measuring 27°, 162°, and 171°.

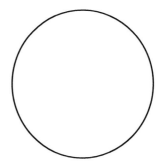

Name:_____ Date: _____

Using a Protractor Like a Pro

> A **right angle** measures 90°. Any angle less than a right angle is an **acute angle**. Any angle greater than a right angle and less than a straight angle is called an **obtuse angle**.

Directions: Use a protractor to measure the angles below. Then, write whether the angle is a *right angle*, an *acute angle*, or an *obtuse angle*.

❶

The angle is _____.

It is a(n) _____ angle.

❷

The angle is _____.

It is a(n) _____ angle.

❸

The angle is _____.

It is a(n) _____ angle.

❹

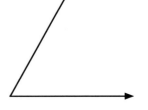

The angle is _____.

It is a(n) _____ angle.

Name:_____ Date: _____

Sketching an Angle

Directions: Use a protractor and a ruler to draw each angle.

❶

Draw an 80° angle.

❷

Draw a 105° angle.

❸

Draw a 45° angle.

❹

Draw a 120° angle.

❺

Draw a 175° angle.

❻

Draw a 15° angle.

Name: _____ Date: _____

180 is the Magic Number

All triangles have three angles that always add up to 180°.

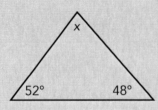

$x + 52° + 48° = 180°$

$x + 100° = 180°$

$x + 100° - 100° = 180° - 100°$

$x = 80°$

Directions: Given the known angles for each triangle, find the missing angle.
Hint: All triangles have a total of 180°.

❶

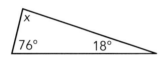

_____ + _____ + _____ = 180°   x = _____

❷

_____ + _____ + _____ = 180°   x = _____

❸

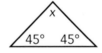

_____ + _____ + _____ = 180°   x = _____

❹

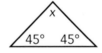

_____ + _____ + _____ = 180°   x = _____

Name:_____ Date: _____

More Than a Simple Dot or Line

A **point** is an object without dimension that marks a location. It is usually labeled by a capital letter.

A **line** is a set of points having direction. The number of points can be infinite. A line has one dimension. This line is labeled $\overleftrightarrow{AB}$.

A   B

A **line segment** is a line with two end points. This line segment is labeled $\overline{AB}$.

A   B

A **ray** is a line with one end point that goes to infinity. This ray is labeled $\overrightarrow{AB}$.

A   B

Directions: Create a line, line segment, or ray in the boxes below.

❶	❷
line FG	ray DE
❸	❹
line segment UV	ray CD

Name:_____ Date: _____

Line, Line Segment, or Ray?

Directions: Look at the lines, line segments, and rays. Label each object.

1

C●————————————●D

_____

2

←————●————————————●
      P   Q

_____

3

A●————B●————→

_____

4

X●————————————●→
              Y

_____

5

A●
   ＼
    ＼
     B●
      ＼→

_____

6

        ●→
       U
←●————————
 T

_____

Name:_____ Date: _____

Drawing Perpendicular and Parallel Lines

Perpendicular lines are lines that intersect at right angles.

Parallel lines are always the same distance apart and never intersect.

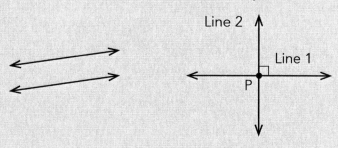

Parallel lines   Perpendicular lines

Directions: Draw each object described below.

---

❶ Draw perpendicular line segments CD and DE.

---

❷ Draw parallel line segments UV and WX.

---

❸ Draw perpendicular line segments JK and KL.

---

❹ Draw parallel line segments MN and OP.

Name:_____ Date: _____

Shape Up! Identifying Shapes

Directions: Answer the questions. Use words from the Word Bank.

Word Bank

equilateral triangle	heptagon	irregular polygon
isosceles triangle	octagon	hexagon
parallelogram	rectangle	quadrilateral
regular polygon		

1 What shape has eight sides and eight angles? _____

2 What shape has three sides, two of which are equal in length?

_____

3 What are all shapes called that are four-sided figures?

_____

4 What shape has two sets of parallel lines with different lengths and four

right angles? _____

5 What shape has three equal sides and three equal angles?

_____

6 What is a two-dimensional shape that has equal sides and equal angles?

_____

7 What shape has six sides and six angles? _____

8 What shape can have two obtuse angles and two acute angles?

_____

9 What shapes has seven sides? _____

10 What is a two-dimensional shape that does not have equal sides or equal

angles? _____

Name:_____ Date: _____

Right Triangles and Right Angles

> A **right triangle** is a triangle with one angle that is a **right angle** measuring 90 degrees.
>
>

Directions: Look at the triangles. Circle the triangles that are right triangles.

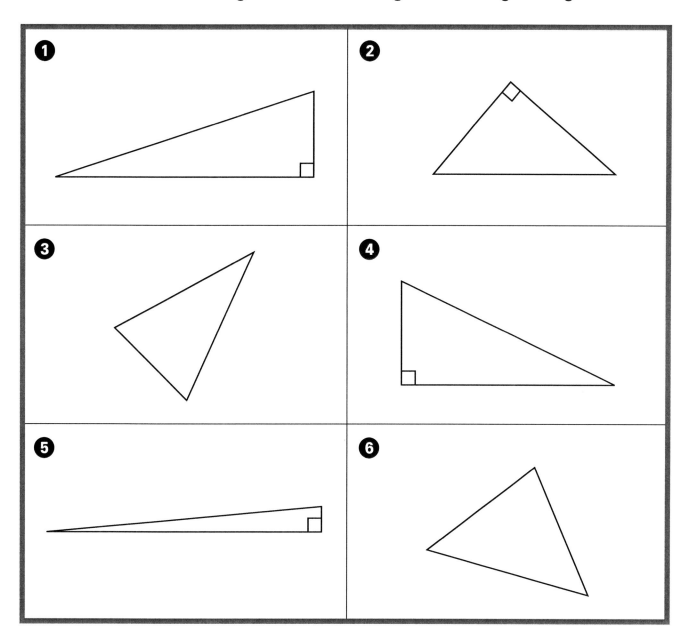

Right Triangles and Right Angles *(cont.)*

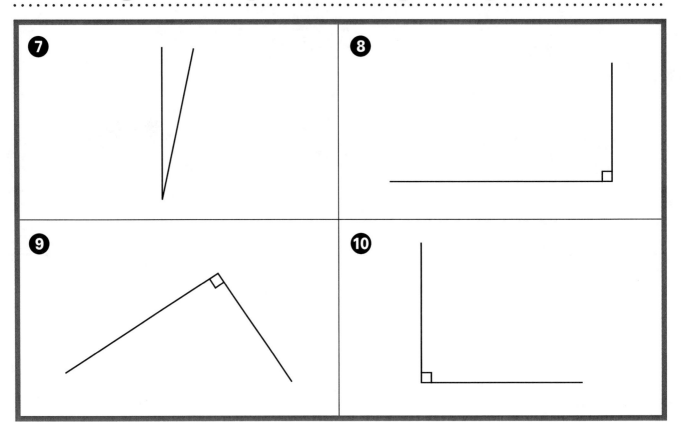

Name:_____ Date: _____

Identifying Lines of Symmetry

Symmetry occurs when two halves of a figure mirror each other across a dividing line.

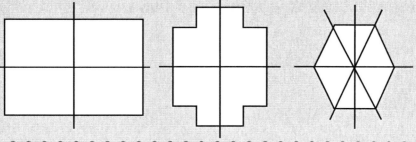

Directions: Draw lines to show the symmetry of the following figures. Draw as many symmetry lines as you can find accurately.

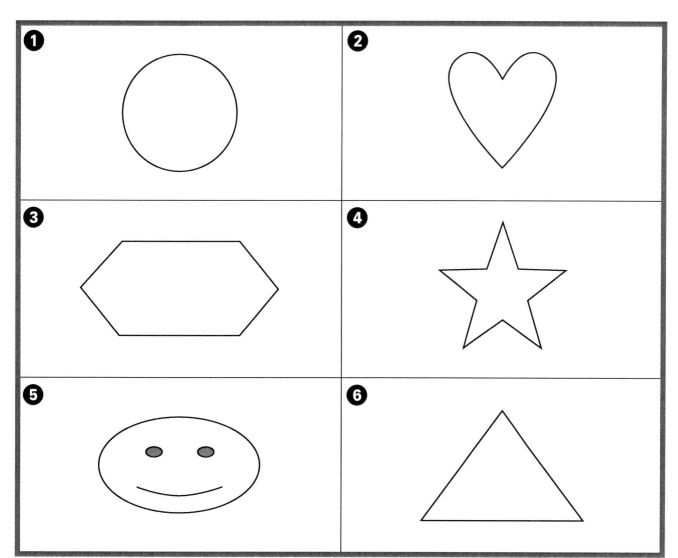

Name:_____ Date: _____

Symmetry or Not?

Directions: Decide whether the shapes are symmetrical. For shapes that have lines of symmetry, draw them on the shape.

1

_____

2

_____

3

_____

4

_____

5

_____

6

_____

7

_____

8

_____

9

_____

10

_____

References Cited

Annis, L. F., and D. B. Annis. 1987. *Does practice make perfect? The effects of repetition on student learning.* Paper presented at the annual meeting of the American Educational Research Association, Washington, DC.

Marzano, R. 2010. When practice makes perfect...sense. *Educational Leadership* (68):81–83.

National Governors Association Center for Best Practices and Council of Chief State School Officers. 2010. Common core standards. http://www.corestandards.org/the-standards.

Answer Key

Breaking Up Words (page 11)

1. en-gine
2. wea-ther
3. ca-stle
4. quick-ly
5. creep-ing
6. foot-ball
7. a-round
8. sun-set
9. door-bell
10. ex-tra
11. tick-et
12. be-neath

Word Division (page 12)

1. a-chieve
2. pro-duct
3. ca-pi-tal
4. sea-son
5. fac-tor-y
6. wet-land
7. ex-plore
8. gen-der
9. cit-y
10. e-con-o-my

More Word Division (page 13)

Students' answers will vary.

Decoding Strategies for New Words (page 14)

Students' answers will vary.

It's All Relative: Using Relative Pronouns (page 15)

1. that
2. who
3. whose
4. which
5. whom
6. which

Writing with Relative Pronouns (page 16)

Students' answers will vary but they should use the relative pronoun listed within their answers.

Finding Relative Pronouns in Literature (page 17)

Students' answers will vary.

Adverbs Tell Us More About the Action (page 18)

1. why
2. where
3. when
4. when
5. why
6. when, when
7. where
8. why

Making Relative Adverbs Personal (page 19)

Students' answers will vary, but they should use the relative adverb within their answers.

Alternatives to Using Relative Adverbs? (page 20)

Students' answers will vary.

Progressive Verbs (page 21)

1. will be playing
2. was climbing
3. will be sleeping
4. is giving
5. will be writing
6. was eating
7. will be running
8. is standing

Showing Progression Through Pictures (page 22)

Students' examples will vary but should reflect the progressive form of a verb listed within each box.

Verbs: Writing Progressive Forms (page 23)

Students' answers will vary.

Getting into Modal Auxiliary Verbs (page 24)

Students' answers will vary.

Adding the Auxiliaries (page 25)

Answers may vary. The following are some suggestions:

1. must
2. can
3. may
4. ought to
5. can
6. will
7. may
8. might

Answer Key *(cont.)*

Putting Adjectives in Order (page 26)

1. There was a disgusting, small, black spider hanging from the web in the corner of the room.
2. The sweet, tall, old man came to the door and asked what we wanted.
3. Those fancy, black, leather shoes are way too small for me now.
4. The gorgeous, small, yellow daffodil flowers are in a vase on my table.
5. The night was quiet when the spooky, large, brown barn owl began to hoot.

Writing Sequenced Adjectives (page 27)

Students' sentences will vary but should include the adjectives listed in the correct order.

Adjectives Complete the Story (page 28)

Students' answers will vary but should include adjectives to complete the story.

It's Just a Phrase: Prepositional Phrases (page 29)

Answers may vary. The following are some suggestions:

1. The yarn is below the cat.
2. The raincoat is on the girl.
3. The soil is under the girl.
4. The helmet is on her head.

Writing Prepositional Phrases (page 30)

Answers may vary. The following are some suggestions:

1. A cow can be seen wearing a bell under his neck.
2. The baby is holding the rattle under her blanket.
3. The airplane is on the runway.
4. Her sock is between her foot and her shoe.
5. The flag is on the building.
6. The scoop of ice cream is on the cone.
7. The farmer is between the field and the barn.
8. The scarf was placed below the snowman's head.

More on the Preposition (page 31)

Students' sentences will vary, but should include the preposition provided.

Complete That Sentence! (page 32)

1. I
2. C
3. I
4. I
5. C
6. I
7. C
8. I
9. C
10. C

Students' sentences will vary.

Answer Key *(cont.)*

Stop That Run-on Sentence (page 33)

Answers may vary. The following are some suggestions:

1. My books are on the table. My math book is on top.
2. They were closing the store. It was time to go home.
3. Watch out for the slippery ice! You could fall and hurt yourself.
4. I got a new blue dress. The blue shoes match perfectly.
5. My brother made the team. Will I be able to play baseball some day?

Piecing Together Sentence Fragments (page 34)

Answers may vary. The following are some suggestions:

1. The tennis ball went flying in the air.
2. My best friend threw a surprise party for me!
3. Manny's birthday party turned out to be a complete success!
4. Grandma's favorite flower pot fell off the fence.
5. The girl was blowing big bubbles.
6. A giant spider made its way through the house!
7. The piglet ran into the street!
8. It took several minutes before anyone realized that her hamster went missing.

Essential Apostrophes: They're, You're, and It's (page 35)

1. It's
2. You're
3. There
4. their
5. its
6. your
7. they're
8. It's, your

To, Too, or Two? (page 36)

1. I'm going *to* be in a dance recital tomorrow. I'll be wearing my new tutu, which is a little *too* big. *Two* of my friends will dance, *too*.

   I'm *too* excited *to* sleep, but I have *to* go *to* bed.

2. The leaves were falling from the trees as I walked *to* school. It must be fall, which I call autumn, *too*. I know that there are *two* more weeks until Halloween. I can't wait *to* go trick or treating! My friend Alexa is going *to* walk with me, *too*. We will remember *to* say "Thank You!" after we get our candy. I hope that I get at least *two* lollipops to eat!

Spell It Out Correctly (page 37)

Students' sentences will vary, but should include the homophone used correctly.

Capital with a C (page 38)

1. When I went to the store, I saw Mrs. Cooper buying strawberries.
2. My family will go to Disneyland in July.
3. I am reading *Old Yeller* this week.
4. My sister, Sarah, says her favorite holiday is Halloween.
5. On Thursday, we will celebrate Thanksgiving.
6. Our neighbor is a cheerleader at Roosevelt High School.
7. In August, we are going to visit Aunt Margaret in San Francisco, California.
8. My friend, Rosa, went to Springfield and I went to New York City.
9. My little brother had to see Dr. May for an ear infection.
10. Dad was not happy that I was late getting home.

Special Titles Deserve Special Letters (page 39)

Students' answers will vary.

Answer Key *(cont.)*

Answering with Capitals (page 40)

Students' answers will vary.

"What's That You Say?" (page 41)

1. "Why is the principal coming in our room?" Mrs. Carter's students wondered.

2. Hector teased, "You are going to be in last place."

3. "Please hang up your backpacks," Mr. Fox called out, "before you sit at your desk."

4. "Where is the ice cream social being held tonight?" my mom asked me after school.

5. Jason shouted, "I am not happy about my soccer team's loss!"

6. "I don't think I can come to your party," Fiona told me, "because I have a family gathering to go to."

7. "What animals would you expect to see in the Amazon rain forest?" Mrs. Garcia asked.

8. The teacher commented, "When we study space you will learn about comets and meteors."

Quoting and Punctuating (page 42)

1. Michael shouted, "Let's get busy with the paint!"

2. "Has anyone in this group ever climbed Mount Everest?" asked the mountain guide.

3. Mr. Cumming said, "Please watch your step through the pond."

Conjunction Commas (page 43)

1. We went to a great concert last night, but the music was too loud.

2. George likes to play soccer during recess, and his friend Adam likes to play baseball.

3. The fire raged on all through the night, so the firemen felt exhausted by the break of the day.

4. Raymond had trouble sleeping that night, for the next day was his birthday.

Adding Commas to the List (page 44)

1. All birds have feathers, wings, and beaks.

2. My sister is hungry, sleepy, and grumpy.

3. I ordered a pizza with pepperoni, mushrooms, and olives.

4. This rule applies to Jake, Cindia, and yourself.

5. Lily would have finished her homework, but she had a late soccer practice, and fell asleep early.

6. My dog has brown spots, a short tail, and fuzzy feet.

7. The birthday party was planned for the park, but it was rainy that day, and my mom decided that indoors was better.

8. Can you go to the store and get butter, flour, and milk?

9. When I go on vacation, I am taking a suitcase, my bike, and a camera.

10. Did your friend want a book, clothes, or a DVD for her birthday?

Dictionary Definitions (page 45)

Sentences will vary. Definitions may vary.

sinister: threatening or suggesting harm

plague: a disease that spreads very rapidly

distraught: extremely upset and distressed

atmosphere: the air or climate in a given place

A Friendly Dictionary (page 46)

Students' answers will vary.

Answer Key *(cont.)*

Show Me, Don't Tell Me (page 47)

Answers may vary. The following are some suggestions:

1. I was sound asleep when all of a sudden my puppy snuck up to me and rested her head against my torso. The whimpering sounds she made and the batting of her eyelashes, made me realize that she was ready to be fed.

2. It was raining cats and dogs! Luckily, Mrs. Green let me borrow her umbrella so I wouldn't get drenched as I was waiting for my dad to pick me up.

3. My parents' search for the perfect home finally came to an end. This weekend, we stumbled across a beautiful two-story house. The windows were boarded up and there was a sign that read, "No trespassing." The lock on the door indicated that the house was empty.

4. As I sat at the dining room table, frustrated that I couldn't figure out how to put my puzzle together, my little brother handed me a piece that had fallen to the ground.

Vivid Verbs: Using Descriptive Words (page 48)

Answers may vary. The following are some suggestions:

1. The audience chanted, "More! More! More!" for the band to return to the stage.

2. The dog sprinted as he tugged his owner around the block.

3. Simon threw a tantrum at the store. He wanted an ice cream cone right now!

4. The girls skipped towards the pool.

Description Riddles (page 49)

Riddle #1: a sun
Riddle #2: an elevator
Riddle #3: a soccer ball

The Order in the Phrase (page 50)

Students' revised sentences will vary.

Powerful Ending Punctuation (page 51)

1. What happened to the girl who broke her leg during the soccer game? (interrogative)

2. The team was so worried about her after watching her cry. (declarative)

3. Please be careful, everyone! (exclamatory)

4. The team gathered to have a snack after the game and greet their opponents. (declarative)

5. How did the other team feel that one of our players got hurt? (interrogative)

6. Our coaches talked with us about what it means to show good sportsmanship. (declarative)

Emphasizing Information with Commas (page 52)

1. The blue whale, measuring 98 feet in length, is the largest known animal to have ever existed.

2. The carnival ride, The Spinning Top, can make people sick when it starts moving fast.

3. We went to Richardson Park, a wonderful open space near downtown, to celebrate my birthday.

4. For Valentine's Day, my dad gave me my favorite treat.

5. My brother, the world's most annoying six-year-old, would not stop bothering me this morning.

6. The United States of America, our great nation, will celebrate its birthday on the Fourth of July.

7. The Amazon Rainforest, the most magnificent place in the world, is home to thousands of interesting plant and animal species.

8. The plane we are taking, a 747, will have plenty of room.

Answer Key (cont.)

Emphasizing Information with Commas (cont.) (page 52)

9. The day after my party, Kevin called to apologize for missing out on the fun.
10. The referee, after consulting with other officials on the field, called a penalty on the player.

Parenthetical Expressions (page 53)

Students' answers will vary but should include the usage of parenthetical expressions.

Punctuating a Paragraph (page 54)

Dear Grandma,

Thank you so much for sending me the wonderful birthday present! How did you know that I needed a green sweater? It even came from my favorite store. I had a wonderful day! My friend, Lily, helped my parents throw me a surprise party. Of course, I had no idea. I was so shocked, to say the least. My parents and my friends made me feel like the luckiest girl!

I hope I get to see you soon. It's been too long, I think.

Love,

Katy

Formal vs. Informal: When to Choose a Writing Style (page 55)

Students' answers will vary.

Practicing Informal and Formal Writing (page 56)

Students' answers will vary. One paragraph should be written in an informal style. The other paragraph should be written in a formal style.

Making Inferences in Daily Life (page 57)

Answers may vary. The following are some suggestions:

1. The bus got into an accident, or perhaps the bus is delayed because of other accidents.
2. The park ranger is lighting a campfire and celebrating the end of the summer season.
3. There is a power outage.

Explicit Details and Implicit Inferences (page 58)

Students' answers will vary.

The Big Idea (page 59)

1. football field
2. towels
3. hairy
4. leaf
5. New York
6. sky
7. television
8. shoe
9. diving board
10. pizza

A Paragraph's Main Idea (page 60)

Main Idea: Animals either have backbones or they do not.

Supporting Details: Invertebrates do not have backbones. Vertebrates do have backbones. Mammals are vertebrates.

What's It All About? (page 61)

Answers may vary. The following are some suggestions:

1. The main idea of the text is that studying fossils is how scientists learn about life in the past.
2. Scientists study rocks to find out how old rocks are. Fossils can be found in rocks that used to be mud millions of years ago.

Identifying Main Idea Graphic Organizer (page 62)

Students' answers will vary.

Answer Key *(cont.)*

Summarizing Life Experiences (page 63)

Students' answers will vary.

Explaining by Summarizing (page 64)

Students' answers will vary.

Summarizing Informational Texts (page 65)

Students' answers will vary.

Academic Words in Context (page 66)

1. the order in which things occur
2. an issue that contributes to or has an influence on the result of something
3. an assortment
4. the effect of something on a person or thing

Making Connections to Vocabulary (page 67)

Students' answers will vary.

Comparing and Contrasting Academic Words (page 68)

Answers may vary. The following are some suggestions:

1. A belief leads someone to claim something.
2. A belief is someone's thoughts about something. A claim is stating how someone feels about something.

Vocabulary Diagram (page 69)

Students' vocabulary diagrams will vary.

Chronological Order in Writing (page 70)

1. get up; brush teeth; eat breakfast; go out the door; go to school
2. morning bell rings; morning recess; lunch recess; afternoon bell rings; after-school care begins
3. the players greet each other and wish each other a good game; the referee blows the whistle for the game to begin; halftime; the whistle indicates that the game is over; girls cheer the other team and enjoy an after-game snack

Determining Text Order (page 71)

1. You first mix warm water and yeast in a large bowl.
2. You add the salt, oil, and flour.
3. You let the yeast do its magic and allow the bread to rise for one hour.
4. first, next, then, finally, when you are all done

Mapping a Chronological Text (page 72)

Students' answers will vary.

Comparing and Contrasting Two Topics (page 73)

Students' answers will vary, but should include similarities and differences between the given topics.

Tale of Two Documents (page 74)

Answers may vary. The following are some suggestions:

1. a. Both documents continue to shape life in America today.

   b. Both documents were created in the early days of America's existence.
2. a. The documents were written and signed by different people on different days.

   b. The documents address different issues.

Make Your Own Comparisons (page 75)

Students' answers will vary but should include comparisons between two informational texts.

Solving Problems (page 76)

Students' answers will vary.

Answer Key (cont.)

Solutions in Editorials (page 77)

Answers may vary. The following are some suggestions:

1. The cafeteria is serving food on Styrofoam trays with plastic utensils. The materials are not very environmentally friendly.
2. The school district is creating a lot of unnecessary waste. It's not good for the environment.

Problem/Solution Patterns in Texts (page 78)

Students' answers will vary.

Firsthand Versus Secondhand Accounts (pages 79–81)

Students' answers will vary.

Learning from Charts (pages 82–83)

1. obsidian
2. sedimentary rock
3. A table organizes the information and makes it easy to read and to compare.
4. A table is a great way to show information to readers in a format that makes a comparison easier.

Interpreting Charts on Your Own (page 84)

Students' answers will vary.

Understanding Graphs in Informational Texts (pages 85–86)

1. 70 days
2. potatoes and tomatoes
3. The graph helps readers to compare information about growing times for vegetables.
4. It is much easier to read this information in a graph that usually shows the comparisons rather than reading a paragraph.

Reading Diagrams (pages 87–88)

Students' answers will vary.

Understanding Timelines (page 89)

1. 1732
2. 67 years old
3. 8 years
4. Answers will vary.

Mapping Out a Timeline (page 90)

Students' answers will vary.

An Author's Use of Evidence (pages 91–92)

Students' answers will vary.

Where's the Evidence? (page 93)

Students' answers will vary.

Word Sleuths: Finding Context Clues (page 94)

1. antonym
2. direct definition
3. synonym

Synonyms or Antonyms: Using Context Clues (page 95)

1. presumed
2. different
3. tell the difference
4. related
5. end
6. expected ahead of time
7. put together
8. expressive and articulate

Explanations and Examples: Unraveling Clues in Context (page 96)

1. void and cancelled
2. gradual change
3. went before
4. tense excitement
5. quickly act something out
6. philosophy
7. break out

Answer Key (cont.)

Tracking Context Clues (page 97)

Students' answers will vary.

The Root of the Word (page 98)

Word	Prefix	Root	Suffix
1. import	im	port	
2. prepay	pre	pay	
3. likeable		like	able
4. loyalty		loyal	ty
5. autopilot	auto	pilot	
6. telegram	tele	gram	
7. biology		bio	logy
8. nonstop	non	stop	
9. international	inter	nation	al
10. telephone	tele	phone	

Root for the Word! (page 99)

1. study of the Earth
2. to write a copy
3. to throw in between
4. to carry away
5. a way to travel underground
6. study of life

Grouping Together the Word Parts (page 100)

Students' answers will vary.

Adding on to the Root (page 101)

1. dialogue
2. portable
3. autograph
4. geologist
5. microscope
6. subway

Using a Dictionary (page 102)

Students' answers will vary.

Support Your Writing with a Dictionary (page 103)

Students' answers will vary.

New Words in the Thesaurus (page 104)

Students' answers will vary.

As Smart as a What? Identifying Similes (page 105)

Students' answers will vary.

Comparison Writing with Similes (page 106)

Students' answers will vary.

Vivid Descriptions with Metaphors (page 107)

Students' answers will vary.

Emotional Metaphors: Comparing Emotions to Many Things (page 108)

Students' answers will vary.

What's That Idiom? (page 109)

1. c
2. b
3. e
4. j
5. i
6. g
7. a
8. h
9. f
10. d

Writing with Idioms (page 110)

Students' sentences will vary but should include the idiom.

Listen to that Old Adage (page 111)

Students' sentences will vary.

Passing on the Wisdom (page 112)

Students' sentences will vary.

Inferring From a Picture (page 113)

Students' answers will vary.

Explicit vs. Implicit Details (pages 114–115)

1. explicit
2. implicit
3. implicit
4. explicit
5. implicit
6. explicit
7. explicit
8. implicit
9. implicit
10. explicit

Answer Key *(cont.)*

Practice Making Inferences (page 116)

Answers may vary. The following are some suggestions:

1. Jack and Wendy are visiting a carnival.
2. Clues are: dark, spooky, Fun House, and Ferris Wheel
3. It is the Fourth of July.
4. Clues are: sky lit up with each boom, spectacular show, warm summer night, light performance in the sky.

Inferences in Text (page 117)

Students' answers will vary.

Discovering the Theme (pages 118–119)

Answers may vary. The following are some suggestions:

1. The theme is that being honest is always the best plan.
2. Evidence might be that Nina decided to lie because she was afraid of failing the test. She didn't tell her parents the truth. She ended up missing out on a fun day because she wasn't truthful.

Comparing Themes To Experiences (page 120)

Students' answers will vary.

Book Theme Graphic Organizer (page 121)

Students' answers will vary.

A Character Web (page 122)

Students' answers will vary.

Identifying Character Development (page 123)

Students' answers will vary.

Writing a Character Sketch (page 124)

Students' answers will vary.

Setting Survey (page 125)

Students' answers will vary.

Comparing Settings (page 126)

Students' answers will vary.

An Ideal Setting (page 127)

Students' answers will vary.

Events That Build (page 128)

Students' answers will vary.

Ordering Story Events (page 129)

Students' answers will vary.

Answer Key (cont.)

What Happens Next? (page 130)

Answers may vary. The following are some suggestions:

Event #1	Event #2	Event #3
A wolf comes to the first house made of straw. He huffs and he puffs and he blows it down. He gobbles up the first little pig.	The wolf comes to the second house made of sticks. He huffs and he puffs and he blows it down. He gobbles up the second little pig.	A wolf comes to the third house made of bricks. He huffs and he puffs, but he can't blow it down. The pig tricks the wolf, who falls down the chimney into a boiling pot of water.

Event #1	Event #2	Event #3
A shepherd boy keeps tricking people in his village by calling out "Wolf!" even though no wolf is there.	When others kept coming to rescue the boy, they saw that there was no wolf. People were frustrated that the boy was tricking them by calling wolf.	When the boy actually sees a wolf who is eating his flock, he calls "Wolf!" but no one believes him and no one comes to help him.

Descriptions from Mythology (pages 131–132)

Students' answers will vary.

Analysis of a Hero or Heroine (pages 133–134)

Students' answers will vary.

A Different Point of View (page 135)

Students' answers will vary.

Changing Your Point of View (page 136)

Students' answers will vary.

Celebrating Around the World (pages 137–138)

Students' answers will vary.

The Importance of Tradition (pages 139–140)

1. One lesson of this tale is that a simple person might surprise you.
2. Answers will vary.
3. This tale might help teach Russian people to not make assumptions about other people.

Common Themes Across Cultures (page 141)

Students' answers will vary.

Oral Reading Checklist (page 142)

Students' answers will vary.

Timed Reading to Build Fluency (page 143)

Students' answers will vary.

What's Your Opinion on That? (page 144)

Students' answers will vary.

All About Me: Writing to Inform (page 145)

Students' answers will vary.

Putting All the Parts Together: Writing Narrative Stories (page 146)

Students' answers will vary.

Editing Checklist (page 147)

Students' answers will vary.

Making the Most of Group Discussions (page 148)

Students' answers will vary.

Answer Key *(cont.)*

Collaboration Includes Many Voices (page 149)

Students' answers will vary.

Comparing Quantities: Showing What Multiplication Means (page 150)

1. Students' drawings and sentences should represent the two quantities listed.
2. Students' drawings and sentences should represent the two quantities listed.

Multiplication Equations (page 151)

1. 5
2. 9
3. 9
4. 7
5. 5
6. 11
7. 13
8. 8
9. 40 is the same as:

   8×5

   10×4

   20×2

   40×1
10. 100 is the same as:

    50×2

    25×4

    10×10

    100×1
11. 12 is the same as:

    6×2

    4×3

    12×1

    2×6
12. 36 is the same as:

    6×6

    9×4

    12×3

    36×1

Does Order Matter? The Commutative Property (page 152)

1. $6 \times 4 = 24$

   $4 \times 6 = 24$
2. $9 \times 8 = 72$

   $8 \times 9 = 72$
3. $7 \times 6 = 42$

   $6 \times 7 = 42$
4. $8 \times 7 = 56$

   $7 \times 8 = 56$
5. $6 \times 5 = 30$

   $5 \times 6 = 30$
6. $4 \times 3 = 12$

   $3 \times 4 = 12$

Using Operations to Solve Word Problems (page 153)

1. $8 \times 2 = 16$ blocks
2. $6 \times 2 = 12$ goals

As Much As What? Solving Word Problems (page 154)

1. $3 \times 7 = 21$
2. $8 \times 6 = 48$
3. $24 \div 6 = 4$
4. $360 \div 36 = 10$

Creating Math Stories (page 155)

Students' word problems will vary but should represent the equation listed.

The Five-Step Plan (page 156)

$\$0.65 \times 2 = \$1.30$; $\$2.00 - \$1.30 = \$.70$; Jack received 70 cents in change.

A Little Bit of Everything: Multistep Word Problems (page 157)

1. Step 1: $12 + 24 + 29 = 65$

   Step 2: $65 - 18 = 47$

   Final Answer: Sergio has 47 stamps left.
2. Step 1: $3 + 6 = 9$

   Step 2: $20 - 9 = 11$

   Final Answer: Lily has to eat 11 for dessert.
3. Step 1: $7 \times 3 = 21$

   Step 2: $24 - 21 = 3$

   Final Answer: There is enough pizza. There will be 3 slices left over.
4. Step 1: $\$0.75 + \$1.50 = \$2.25$

   Step 2: $\$2.25 - \$2.00 = \$0.25$

   Final Answer: Parker does have enough money. He will get 25 cents in change.

Answer Key (cont.)

Solve That Letter: Unknown Quantities (page 158)

Students' steps will vary. The following are the answers:

1. $y = 10$ **2.** $x = 9$ **3.** $x = 45$

Fun with Factor Pairs! (page 159)

1. 30: 30 and 1;10 and 3; 6 and 5; 15 and 2
2. 24: 24 and 1; 12 and 2; 6 and 4; 8 and 3
3. 16: 16 and 1; 8 and 2; 4 and 4
4. 42: 42 and 1; 21 and 2; 3 and 14; 6 and 7
5. 88: 88 and 1; 44 and 2; 22 and 4; 11 and 8
6. 50: 50 and 1; 25 and 2; 10 and 5
7. 66: 66 and 1; 33 and 2; 22 and 3; 11 and 6
8. 72: 72 and 1; 36 and 2; 24 and 3; 18 and 4; 12 and 6; 9 and 8

Minding the Multiples (page 160)

1. 15
2. 28
3. 30
4. 64
5. 81
6. 84
7. 30
8. 18
9. 10: 10, 20, 30, 40, 50
10. 8: 8, 16, 24, 32, 40
11. 6: 6, 12, 18, 24, 30
12. 11: 11, 22, 33, 44, 55

Prime or Composite? (page 161)

1. composite   **4.** prime
2. prime   **5.** prime
3. composite   **6.** composite

More Prime or Composite? (page 162)

1. 2, 2, 11
2. 3, 3, 2, 2
3. 2, 2, 5, 5
4. 7, 3, 3
5. 2, 3, 3
6. 3, 3, 2, 2, 2

What's the Rule? (page 163)

1. 7, 14, 21, 28, 35, 42, 49
Pattern Rule: multiples of 7 or adding 7
2. 1, 4, 7, 10, 13, 16, 19
Pattern Rule: adding 3
3. 1, 2, 5, 10, 17, 26, 37, 50
Pattern Rule: adding odd numbers (1, 3, 5, 7, 9, 11, 13)
4. 63, 54, 45, 36, 27, 18, 9, 0
Pattern Rule: subtracting 9 from previous number
5. 1, 1, 2, 3, 5, 8, 13, 21, 34
Pattern Rule: adding the two previous numbers
6. 1, 3, 7, 13, 21, 31, 43, 57
Pattern Rule: adding even numbers (2, 4, 6, 8, 10, 12, 14)

Noticing Patterns in Numbers (page 164)

1. 11, 22, 33, 44, 55, 66, 77, 88, 99, 110, 121
What is the rule for this pattern? + 11
2. 5, 10, 15, 20, 25, 30, 35, 40, 45, 50, 55
What is the rule for this pattern? + 5
3. 3, 6, 9, 12, 15, 18, 21, 24, 27, 30, 33
What is the rule for this pattern? + 3

Answer Key (cont.)

Patterns in Function Tables (page 165)

1.

x + 4 = y	
x	y
6	10
8	12
25	29

2.

4x = y	
x	y
5	20
9	36
12	48

3.

x ÷ 3 = y	
x	y
6	2
45	15
18	6

4.

x − 20 = y	
x	y
40	20
264	244
59	39

Expanded Form (page 166)

1. $624 \times 10 = 6{,}240$
2. $92 \times 100 = 9{,}200$
3. $43 \times 100 = 4{,}300$
4. $712 \times 10 = 7{,}120$

Comparing the Places of Value (page 167)

1. 5 thousands = 50 hundreds; 5,000
2. 6 hundreds = 60 tens; 600
3. 20 ones = 2 tens; 20
4. 270 tens = 27 hundreds; 2,700
5. 35.6 thousands = 356 hundreds; 35,600
6. 870 ones = 87 tens; 870
7. 910 ones = 91 tens; 910
8. 8 thousands = 80 hundreds; 8,000

Dividing the Places (page 168)

1. $930 \div 10 = 93$
2. $1{,}000 \div 100 = 10$
3. $220 \div 10 = 22$
4. $6{,}700 \div 100 = 67$
5. $45{,}000 \div 1{,}000 = 45$
6. $90 \div 10 = 9$

Fill in the Blank Values (page 169)

1. $4{,}500 \div 10 = 450$
2. $100 \times 82 = 8{,}200$
3. $300 \div 10 = 30$
4. $62 \times 10 = 620$
5. $85{,}000 \div 1{,}000 = 85$
6. $770 \div 10 = 77$
7. $4 \times 10 = 40$
8. $550 \div 10 = 55$
9. $1{,}800 \div 18 = 100$
10. $990 \times 10 = 9{,}900$
11. $220 \div 10 = 22$
12. $12 \times 100 = 1{,}200$
13. $2{,}000 \div 1{,}000 = 2$
14. $6 \times 1{,}000 = 6{,}000$
15. $2{,}340 \times 10 = 23{,}400$
16. $5{,}000 \div 100 = 50$

Answer Key (cont.)

Reading and Writing Numbers (page 170)

1. one thousand one
2. seventy-five
3. six hundred twenty-one
4. four hundred fifty-three
5. thirty-three
6. ninety
7. two thousand fifty-six
8. 6,050
9. 2,842
10. 8,069
11. 1,500
12. 6,453

Expanding on Expanded Form (page 171)

1. six thousand four hundred seventy-six
2. eight thousand five hundred forty-one
3. two thousand nine hundred fifty-nine
4. four hundred forty-four
5. one thousand eighty-two
6. nine thousand five hundred sixty
7. three thousand ninety-nine
8. five thousand one hundred ten
9. 8,043
10. 8,943
11. 3,893
12. 1,083

Comparing Many Digits (page 172)

1. <	5. >	9. <	13. >
2. <	6. >	10. >	14. >
3. >	7. =	11. >	15. =
4. <	8. <	12. <	16. <

High Places to Low Places (page 173)

1. 3,101   3,100   311   310
2. 6,600   661   660   600
3. 710   700   77   70
4. 4,404   4,400   444   441
5. 505   500   55   50
6. 111   110   101   100

Rounding Up and Rounding Down (page 174)

1. 90	4. 80	7. 310
2. 450	5. 290	8. 150
3. 90	6. 70	

What's A-Round 100? (page 175)

1. 700	8. 1,300
2. 300	9. 200
3. 9,000	10. 1,200
4. 8,200	11. 8,300
5. 100	12. 500
6. 2,900	13. 2,300
7. 400	14. 1,800

A Thousand Times More Fun (page 176)

1. 3,000	7. 13,000
2. 9,000	8. 7,000
3. 2,000	9. 2,000
4. 10,000	10. 20,000
5. 8,000	11. 4,000
6. 5,000	12. 11,000

Round 'Em Up and Out! (page 177)

1. b	3. a	5. b
2. a	4. d	6. d

Steps to Addition (page 178)

1. 152	3. 610	5. 268
2. 49	4. 665	6. 252

Taking More Steps to Add (page 179)

1. 2,396	6. 67,075
2. 34,400	7. 1,077
3. 585	8. 5,188
4. 36,275	9. 24,644
5. 907	10. 29,176

Answer Key *(cont.)*

Take it Away: Subtraction Practice (page 180)

1. 4,286
2. 740
3. 16
4. 5,484
5. 4,953
6. 2,000
7. 92
8. 5,010
9. 4,444

Follow That Symbol! (page 181)

1. $70.68
2. 22,667
3. 37,599
4. 39,077
5. $125.99
6. 274
7. 8,136
8. 88,402
9. $47.02
10. 47,764
11. $66.76
12. 34,574
13. 107,764
14. 1,106
15. 818,421

Place Value and Word Problems (page 182)

1. $755 + 714 + 660 + 586 = 2{,}715$ home runs altogether
2. $800 - 563 = 237$ millimeters

More Practice with Place Value (page 183)

1. $92 + 87 + 82 = 261$ kids in grades K–2
2. $12 + 48 + 32 + 25 = 117$ pounds altogether

Finding Your Own Place (page 184)

Students' answers will vary.

Getting to the Bottom of Multiplication (page 185)

1. 2,449
2. 972
3. 1,848
4. 1,885
5. 1,197
6. 1,220
7. 1,020
8. 2,268
9. 1,512

Multiplying Multiple Digits (page 186)

1. 1,845
2. 1,284
3. 738
4. 860
5. 7,384
6. 1,490
7. 2,392
8. 3,894
9. 1,686
10. 1,530

Practicing Math with Equivalent Measurements (page 187)

1. $6 \times 365 = 2{,}190$ days
2. $60 \times 60 = 3{,}600$ seconds
3. $3{,}600 \times 24 = 86{,}400$ seconds
4. $42 \times 60 = 2{,}520$ minutes

Multiplication Body Facts (page 188)

1. $90 \times 60 = 5{,}400$ beats per hour
2. $4 \times 60 \times 24 = 5{,}760$ quarts per day
3. $960 \times 16 = 15{,}360$ blinks
4. $31 \times 3 = 93$ sneezes

Multiply for Answers (page 189)

1. 1,500 eggs
2. 288 boxes
3. 672 markers
4. 900 necklaces
5. 416 wheels
6. 924 books

What's the Missing Factor? (page 190)

1. 215
2. 49
3. 608
4. 514
5. 708
6. 20
7. 420
8. 37
9. 960
10. 57

Finding Both Missing Factors (page 191)

1. $942 \times 2 = 1884$; $628 \times 3 = 1884$; $471 \times 4 = 1884$; $314 \times 6 = 1884$
2. $873 \times 4 = 3492$; $582 \times 6 = 3492$; $388 \times 9 = 3492$
3. $525 \times 3 = 1575$; $315 \times 5 = 1575$; $225 \times 7 = 1575$; $175 \times 9 = 1575$

Dividing It Up (page 192)

1. 8
2. 11
3. 21
4. 23
5. 107
6. 67
7. 52
8. 15
9. 17

What's Remaining? (page 193)

1. 10 R4
2. 4 R3
3. 16
4. 21 R3
5. 14 R4
6. 7 R1
7. 108
8. 14 R1
9. 25

Answer Key *(cont.)*

Multiplication and Division Connection (page 194)

1. 10 R2   3. 112 R3   5. 197
2. 8 R6   4. 20 R4   6. 84 R1

Mystery Division Problems (page 195)

1. $x = 3$ 5. $x = 8$
2. $x = 15$ 6. $x = 15$
3. $x = 17$ 7. $x = 12$
4. $x = 11$ 8. $x = 25$

Solving Division Word Problems (page 196)

1. Each teacher got 26 popsicles. There were 4 remaining.
2. She can buy 22 candles. She has $2.00 remaining.
3. He can buy 10 packages. There are 3 brushes remaining.
4. He should purchase 65 packages. There are 5 paper towel rolls remaining.

Half Is Half (page 197)

Students' answers will vary, but should show how the fractions are the same using numbers and pictures.

Making Things Equal (page 198)

1. $x = 4$ 4. $x = 2$
2. $x = 2$
3. $x = 3$

Grouping Equivalent Fractions (page 199)

Answers may vary. The following are some suggestions:

1. $\frac{4}{6}, \frac{6}{9}, \frac{8}{12}$ 4. $\frac{18}{20}, \frac{27}{30}, \frac{36}{40}$
2. $\frac{6}{16}, \frac{9}{24}, \frac{12}{32}$ 5. $\frac{16}{26}, \frac{24}{39}, \frac{32}{52}$
3. $\frac{8}{10}, \frac{12}{15}, \frac{16}{20}$

More or Less? Comparing Fractions (page 200)

1. The greater fraction is $\frac{4}{5}$.
2. The greater fraction is $\frac{7}{16}$.

Fraction Evaluation: Measuring Value (page 201)

1. <
2. <
3. <
4. =
5. =
6. >
7. <
8. <

Writing Fraction Word Problems (page 202)

1. Stella's dad ate more. Students' drawings will vary.
2. Students' word problems will vary.

Adding and Subtracting Pieces of the Pie (page 203)

1. $\frac{3}{5}$ 4. $\frac{10}{12}$ or $\frac{5}{6}$
2. $\frac{5}{6}$ 5. $\frac{5}{14}$
3. $\frac{6}{8}$ or $\frac{3}{4}$ 6. $\frac{4}{7}$

More Than a Whole (page 204)

1. $5\frac{5}{8}$ 2. $6\frac{1}{5}$

Breaking Apart a Fraction (page 205)

1. $\frac{1}{8} + \frac{1}{8} + \frac{1}{8} + \frac{1}{8} + \frac{1}{8} + \frac{1}{8} = \frac{6}{8}$
2. $\frac{1}{10} + \frac{1}{10} + \frac{1}{10} + \frac{1}{10} + \frac{1}{10} + \frac{1}{10} + \frac{1}{10} = \frac{7}{10}$
3. $\frac{1}{12} + \frac{1}{12} + \frac{1}{12} + \frac{1}{12} = \frac{4}{12}$

Add Them Up! (page 206)

1. $2\frac{2}{8}$ or $2\frac{1}{4}$ 6. $20\frac{2}{3}$
2. $\frac{6}{7}$ 7. $\frac{4}{5}$
3. $11\frac{2}{6}$ or $11\frac{1}{3}$ 8. $8\frac{1}{4}$
4. $\frac{5}{12}$ 9. $\frac{6}{8}$ or $\frac{3}{4}$
5. $\frac{4}{7}$ 10. $\frac{6}{9}$ or $\frac{2}{3}$

Mixing It Up with Mixed Numbers (page 207)

1. $5\frac{4}{3}$ or $6\frac{1}{3}$ 2. $8\frac{10}{8}$ or $9\frac{2}{8}$ or $9\frac{1}{4}$

266   #50908—Bright & Brainy: 4th Grade Practice   © Shell Education

Answer Key *(cont.)*

Adding Subtraction to the Mix (page 208)
1. $4\frac{3}{6}$ or $4\frac{1}{2}$
2. $2\frac{10}{12}$ or $2\frac{5}{6}$
3. $5\frac{4}{7}$

Adding Mixed Numbers and Whole Numbers (page 209)
1. $9\frac{2}{5}$
2. $10\frac{1}{2}$
3. $18\frac{3}{4}$

Breaking Bread: Solving Fraction Word Problems (page 210)
1. 3 pumpkin muffins
2. 3 wheat bagels

Fraction Solutions (page 211)
1. $6 \times \frac{1}{4}$
2. $8 \times \frac{1}{5}$

Improper Multiplication and Addition (page 212)
1. $\frac{8}{3} = 8 \times \frac{1}{3} = \frac{1}{3} + \frac{1}{3} + \frac{1}{3} + \frac{1}{3} + \frac{1}{3} + \frac{1}{3} + \frac{1}{3} + \frac{1}{3}$
2. $\frac{9}{4} = 9 \times \frac{1}{4} = \frac{1}{4} + \frac{1}{4} + \frac{1}{4} + \frac{1}{4} + \frac{1}{4} + \frac{1}{4} + \frac{1}{4} + \frac{1}{4} + \frac{1}{4}$
3. $\frac{7}{2} = 7 \times \frac{1}{2} = \frac{1}{2} + \frac{1}{2} + \frac{1}{2} + \frac{1}{2} + \frac{1}{2} + \frac{1}{2} + \frac{1}{2}$
4. $\frac{5}{2} = 5 \times \frac{1}{2} = \frac{1}{2} + \frac{1}{2} + \frac{1}{2} + \frac{1}{2} + \frac{1}{2}$
5. $\frac{12}{5} = 12 \times \frac{1}{5} = \frac{1}{5} + \frac{1}{5} + \frac{1}{5} + \frac{1}{5} + \frac{1}{5} + \frac{1}{5} + \frac{1}{5} + \frac{1}{5} + \frac{1}{5} + \frac{1}{5} + \frac{1}{5} + \frac{1}{5}$
6. $\frac{10}{3} = 10 \times \frac{1}{3} = \frac{1}{3} + \frac{1}{3} + \frac{1}{3} + \frac{1}{3} + \frac{1}{3} + \frac{1}{3} + \frac{1}{3} + \frac{1}{3} + \frac{1}{3} + \frac{1}{3}$
7. $\frac{6}{2} = 6 \times \frac{1}{2} = \frac{1}{2} + \frac{1}{2} + \frac{1}{2} + \frac{1}{2} + \frac{1}{2} + \frac{1}{2}$

Fraction Word Problems (page 213)
1. $\frac{3}{4}$
2. $\frac{4}{10}$
3. She used 15 eggs.

Keeping the Order: Multiplying Fractions (page 214)
1. $\frac{6}{2} = 3$
2. $\frac{36}{3} = 13$
3. $\frac{30}{5} = 6$

A Fraction of a Whole Number (page 215)
1. $\frac{15}{9} = 1\frac{6}{9}$
2. $\frac{44}{11} = 4$
3. $\frac{42}{8} = 5\frac{1}{4}$
4. $\frac{12}{4} = 3$

Real World Fractions (page 216)
1. $12 \times \frac{3}{4} = \frac{36}{4} = 9$
2. $24 \times \frac{1}{3} = \frac{24}{3} = 8$
3. $18 \times \frac{2}{3} = \frac{36}{3} = 12$
   6 soccer balls did not make it in.

Fraction Party Riddles (page 217)
1. 10 pounds of rib
2. $7\frac{1}{5}$ pounds of salmon
3. 4 pies

More Fraction Riddles (page 218)
1. $10\frac{6}{15}$ packages or $10\frac{2}{5}$ packages
2. $13\frac{6}{12}$ fruit or $13\frac{1}{2}$ fruit
3. $13\frac{1}{3}$ bags of garbage

Fractions with Tens and Hundreds (page 219)
1. $x = 40$
2. $x = 10$
3. $x = 70$
4. $x = 50$
5. $\frac{10}{10} = 1$
6. $\frac{11}{10} = 1\frac{1}{10}$
7. $\frac{11}{10} = 1\frac{1}{10}$
8. $\frac{14}{10} = 1\frac{4}{10}$

Putting Tens and Hundreds Together (page 220)
1. $\frac{76}{100}$ or $\frac{19}{25}$
2. $\frac{35}{100}$ or $\frac{7}{20}$
3. $\frac{82}{100}$ or $\frac{41}{50}$
4. $\frac{81}{100}$

Turning a Decimal Into a Fraction (page 221)
1. 0.5
2. 0.9
3. 0.2
4. 0.07
5. 0.04
6. 0.26
7. 0.80
8. 0.4
9. 0.06
10. 0.98
11. 0.590
12. 0.1
13. 0.55
14. 0.802

Answer Key *(cont.)*

Getting Decimals in Line (page 222)

1. .5, .25, .09, .07, .06
2. .9, .6, .061, .06, .04
3. .80, .57, .40, .12, .002
4. .9, .57, .090, .02, .006

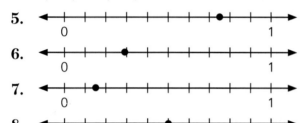

5.
6.
7.
8.

Decimals Large and Small (page 223)

1. >
2. >
3. >
4. =
5. >
6. >
7. >
8. =
9. <
10. >

Measure It Up! (page 224)

1. Students' answers will vary.
2. Students' answers will vary.
3. Students' answers will vary.
4. Students' answers will vary.
5. Students' answers will vary.
6. Students' answers will vary.
7. a
8. a
9. b
10. b

Relative Sizes of Measurement (page 225)

1. meters
2. tons
3. hours
4. fluid ounces
5. minutes
6. pounds
7. centimeters

Equivalent Measurements (pages 226–227)

Inches	Feet
24 in.	2 ft.
48 in.	4 ft.
120 in.	10 ft.
36 in.	3 ft.

Ounces	Pounds
32 oz.	2 lb.
160 oz.	10 lb.
96 oz.	6 lb.
64 oz.	4 lb.

Pints	Quarts
8 pints	4 quarts
40 pints	20 quarts
1,600 pints	800 quarts
900 pints	450 quarts

Minutes	Hours
120 min.	2 hrs.
240 min.	4 hrs.
2,400 min.	40 hrs.
480 min.	8 hrs.

Centimeters	Meters
400 cm	4 m
660 cm	6.6 m
2,400 cm	24 m
800 cm	8 m

Pounds	Tons
8,000 lbs.	4 tons
14,000 lbs.	7 tons
24,000 lbs.	12 tons
40,000 lbs.	20 tons

Cups	Pints
26 cups	13 pints
88 cups	44 pints
80 cups	40 pints
400 cups	200 pints

Answer Key *(cont.)*

Seconds	Minutes
120 sec.	2 min.
1,200 sec.	20 min.
2400 sec.	40 min.
3600 sec.	60 min.

Solving Word Problems (page 228)

1. $\$1.59 \times 20 = \$31.80$
2. $\$64.98 \div 7 = \$9.28$ (One person owes 2 cents more.)
3. $\$219.88 - \$120.80 = \$99.08$
4. $50 \text{ cm} - 42 \text{ cm} = 8 \text{ cm}$
5. $12 \times 2\frac{1}{2} = 30$ inches
6. $9 \times 10 = 90$ mm

Tick Tock Goes the Clock: Elapsed Time Problems (page 229)

1. 6 hours
2. 8:00 pm
3. 8:00 pm
4. 8:45 am
5. 2 hours, 45 minutes
6. 56 minutes

Finding Perimeter: Distance Around a Space (pages 230–231)

1. 60 ft.
2. 22 yd.
3. 22 in.
4. 280 ft.
5. 74 ft.
6. 170 m
7. 180 m
8. 220 ft.

How Large Is Your Area? (pages 232–233)

1. 18 in.^2
2. 35 ft.^2
3. $4,000 \text{ m}^2$
4. $2,500 \text{ cm}^2$
5. 30 ft.^2
6. 616 cm^2

Line Them Up: Making Line Plots (page 234)

1.

```
                          x           x
            x     x    x     x     x              x
    x    x     x    x     x     x     x     x
```
1 in. $1\frac{1}{4}$ in. $1\frac{3}{4}$ in. 2 in. $2\frac{1}{2}$ in. $2\frac{3}{4}$ in. $3\frac{1}{4}$ in. $3\frac{1}{2}$ in.

2. $1\frac{3}{4}$ inches and $2\frac{1}{2}$ inches
3. $3\frac{1}{2}$ inches
4. 1 inch
5. $2\frac{1}{2}$ inches
6. Answers will vary.

Connecting the Dots: Interpreting Data on a Line Plot (page 235)

1. $6\frac{1}{2}$ in.
2. 9 in.
3. 3 in.

Circle Round: Measuring Angles (page 236)

1. 225°
2. 67°

Cutting Through the Circle (page 237)

Students' angles should reflect the angles listed.

Using a Protractor Like a Pro (page 238)

1. 30°; acute angle
2. 90°; right angle
3. 170°; obtuse angle
4. 60°; acute angle

Sketching an Angle (page 239)

Students' angles should reflect the angle listed in each box.

Answer Key (cont.)

180 is the Magic Number (page 240)

1. $x = 86°$ 3. $x = 90°$
2. $x = 103°$ 4. $x = 87°$

More Than a Simple Dot or Line (page 241)

1.
2.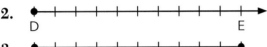
3.
4.

Line, Line Segment, or Ray? (page 242)

1. line segment
2. ray
3. line
4. ray
5. ray
6. line

Drawing Perpendicular and Parallel Lines (page 243)

1.

2.

3.

4.

Shape Up! Identifying Shapes (page 244)

1. octagon
2. isosceles triangle
3. quadrilateral
4. rectangle
5. equilateral triangle
6. regular polygon
7. hexagon
8. parallelogram
9. heptagon
10. irregular polygon

Right Triangles and Right Angles (pages 245–246)

Right Triangles: 1, 2, 4, 5

Right Angles: 8, 9, 10

Identifying Lines of Symmetry (page 247)

1.  Infinite

2.

3.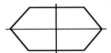

4.

5.

6.

Answer Key *(cont.)*

Symmetry or Not? (page 248)

1. no

2. yes

3. no

4. yes

5. yes

6. yes

7. yes

8. no

9. yes

10. yes

Contents of the Resource CD

Page	Title	Filename
11	Breaking Up Words	breakwords.pdf
12	Word Division	worddivision.pdf
13	More Word Division	moredivision.pdf
14	Decoding Strategies for New Words	decodestrat.pdf
15	It's All Relative: Using Relative Pronouns	allrelative.pdf
16	Writing with Relative Pronouns	writingpro.pdf
17	Finding Relative Pronouns in Literature	relatpronouns.pdf
18	Adverbs Tell Us More About the Action	adverbtaction.pdf
19	Making Relative Adverbs Personal	adverbpersonal.pdf
20	Alternatives to Using Relative Adverbs?	alternadverb.pdf
21	Progressive Verbs	progressverb.pdf
22	Showing Progression Through Pictures	progresspic.pdf
23	Verbs: Writing Progressive Forms	writingforms.pdf
24	Getting into Modal Auxiliary Verbs	modalauxverbs.pdf
25	Adding the Auxiliaries	addingaux.pdf
26	Putting Adjectives in Order	putadjorder.pdf
27	Writing Sequenced Adjectives	writingseqadj.pdf
28	Adjectives Complete the Story	adjstory.pdf
29	It's Just a Phrase: Prepositional Phrases	justaphrase.pdf
30	Writing Prepositional Phrases	writingprep.pdf
31	More on the Preposition	moreonprep.pdf
32	Complete That Sentence!	completesent.pdf
33	Stop That Run-On Sentence	stoprunon.pdf
34	Piecing Together Sentence Fragments	piecefrags.pdf
35	Essential Homophones: They're, You're, and It's	youreits.pdf
36	To, Too, or Two?	totootwo.pdf
37	Spell It Out Correctly	spellcorrect.pdf
38	Capital with a C	capitalc.pdf
39	Special Titles Deserve Special Letters	specialtitle.pdf
40	Answering with Capitals	answercapital.pdf
41	"What's That You Say?"	whatsthatsay.pdf
42	Quoting and Punctuating	quotpunct.pdf
43	Conjunction Commas	conjcomma.pdf
44	Adding Commas to the List	addcommaslist.pdf
45	Dictionary Definitions	dictionarydef.pdf
46	A Friendly Dictionary	frienddict.pdf
47	Show Me, Don't Tell Me	showtell.pdf
48	Vivid Verbs: Using Descriptive Words	vividverb.pdf
49	Description Riddles	descripriddle.pdf
50	The Order in the Phrase	orderphrase.pdf
51	Powerful Ending Punctuation	powerpunct.pdf
52	Emphasizing Information with Commas	infowcomma.pdf
53	Parenthetical Expressions	parenthexp.pdf
54	Punctuating a Paragraph	punctparag.pdf
55	Formal vs. Informal: When to Choose a Writing Style	formalvinf.pdf
56	Practicing Informal and Formal Writing	pracinfformal.pdf
57	Making Inferences in Daily Life	dailylife.pdf
58	Explicit Details and Implicit Inferences	expimplicit.pdf
59	The Big Idea	bigidea.pdf
60	A Paragraph's Main Idea	mainidea.pdf
61	What's It All About?	allabout.pdf
62	Identifying Main Idea Graphic Organizer	mainorganizer.pdf
63	Summarizing Life Experiences	summarlife.pdf

Contents of the Resource CD *(cont.)*

Page	Title	Filename
64	Explaining by Summarizing	explainsum.pdf
65	Summarizing Informational Texts	suminfotexts.pdf
66	Academic Words in Context	wordcontext.pdf
67	Making Connections to Vocabulary	connectvocab.pdf
68	Comparing and Contrasting Academic Words	constrastword.pdf
69	Vocabulary Diagram	vocabdiag.pdf
70	Chronological Order in Writing	orderwrit.pdf
71	Determining Text Order	textorder.pdf
72	Mapping a Chronological Text	maptext.pdf
73	Comparing and Contrasting Two Topics	twotopics.pdf
74	Tale of Two Documents	taletwodocs.pdf
75	Make Your Own Comparisons	owncomp.pdf
76	Solving Problems	solvprob.pdf
77	Solutions in Editorials	soleditorial.pdf
78	Problem/Solution Patterns in Texts	probsolpattern.pdf
79–81	Firsthand Versus Secondhand Accounts	fsaccount.pdf
82–83	Learning from Charts	learningcharts.pdf
84	Interpreting Charts on Your Own	interpretcharts.pdf
85–86	Understanding Graphs in Informational Texts	graphtext.pdf
87–88	Reading Diagrams	readiagram.pdf
89	Understanding Timelines	undertimeline.pdf
90	Mapping Out a Timeline	maptimeline.pdf
91–92	An Author's Use of Evidence	authorevid.pdf
93	Where's the Evidence?	whereedvid.pdf
94	Word Sleuths: Finding Context Clues	wordsleuths.pdf

Page	Title	Filename
95	Synonyms or Antonyms: Using Context Clues	synonymant.pdf
96	Explanations and Examples: Unraveling Clues in Context	unravelclue.pdf
97	Tracking Context Clues	trackclue.pdf
98	The Root of the Word	roottheword.pdf
99	Root for the Word!	roottheword2.pdf
100	Grouping Together the Word Parts	groupwordpart.pdf
101	Adding on to the Root	addingontoroot.pdf
102	Using a Dictionary	usdictionary.pdf
103	Support Your Writing with a Dictionary	supwritdic.pdf
104	New Words in the Thesaurus	newthesaurus.pdf
105	As Smart as a What? Identifying Similes	identsimile.pdf
106	Comparison Writing with Similes	comparsimile.pdf
107	Vivid Descriptions with Metaphors	desmetaphor.pdf
108	Emotional Metaphors: Comparing Emotions to Many Things	emotional.pdf
109	What's That Idiom?	whattidiom.pdf
110	Writing with Idioms	widioms.pdf
111	Listen to that Old Adage	oldadage.pdf
112	Passing on the Wisdom	wisdom.pdf
113	Inferring From a Picture	infpicture.pdf
114–115	Explicit vs. Implicit Details	expdetails.pdf
116	Practice Making Inferences	pracinfer.pdf
117	Inferences in Text	infertext.pdf
118–119	Discovering the Theme	distheme.pdf
120	Comparing Themes To Experiences	comptheme.pdf
121	Book Theme Graphic Organizer	bookorganize.pdf
122	A Character Web	characterweb.pdf

Contents of the Resource CD *(cont.)*

Page	Title	Filename
123	Identifying Character Development	chardevelop.pdf
124	Writing a Character Sketch	charasketch.pdf
125	Setting Survey	setsurvey.pdf
126	Comparing Settings	compset.pdf
127	An Ideal Setting	idealset.pdf
128	Events That Build	eventbuild.pdf
129	Ordering Story Events	orderevents.pdf
130	What Happens Next?	whatnext.pdf
131–132	Descriptions from Mythology	mythology.pdf
133–134	Analysis of a Hero or Heroine	heroheroine.pdf
135	A Different Point of View	differentpov.pdf
136	Changing Your Point of View	changpov.pdf
137–138	Celebrating Around the World	celebworld.pdf
139–140	The Importance of Tradition	imptradition.pdf
141	Common Themes Across Cultures	themeculture.pdf
142	Oral Reading Checklist	oralcheck.pdf
143	Timed Reading to Build Fluency	timedread.pdf
144	What's Your Opinion on That?	youropinion.pdf
145	All About Me: Writing to Inform	allaboutme.pdf
146	Putting All the Parts Together: Writing Narrative Stories	nstories.pdf
147	Editing Checklist	editlist.pdf
148	Making the Most of Group Discussions	gdiscussion.pdf
149	Collaboration Includes Many Voices	collvoices.pdf
150	Comparing Quantities: Showing What Multiplication Means	compquant2.pdf
151	Multiplication Equations	multequations.pdf
152	Does Order Matter? The Commutative Property	doesorder.pdf
153	Using Operations to Solve Word Problems	operations.pdf
154	As Much As What? Solving Word Problems	asmuchwhat.pdf
155	Creating Math Stories	mathstories.pdf
156	The Five-Step Plan	fivestepplan.pdf
157	A Little Bit of Everything: Multistep Word Problems	multiproblem.pdf
158	Solve That Letter: Unknown Quantities	unknownq.pdf
159	Fun with Factor Pairs!	funfactpairs.pdf
160	Minding the Multiples	mindmultip.pdf
161	Prime or Composite?	primecomp.pdf
162	More Prime or Composite?	primecomp2.pdf
163	What's the Rule?	whatrule.pdf
164	Noticing Patterns in Numbers	noticpattern.pdf
165	Patterns in Function Tables	patterntable.pdf
166	Expanded Form	expandform.pdf
167	Comparing the Places of Value	placesvalue.pdf
168	Dividing the Places	dividplaces.pdf
169	Fill in the Blank Values	fillblank.pdf
170	Reading and Writing Numbers	readnums.pdf
171	Expanding on Expanded Form	expanding.pdf
172	Comparing Many Digits	manydigits.pdf
173	High Places to Low Places	highlowplace.pdf
174	Rounding Up and Rounding Down	roundupdown.pdf
175	What's A-Round 100?	whataround.pdf
176	A Thousand Times More Fun	timesmore.pdf
177	Round 'Em Up and Out!	roundout.pdf
178	Steps to Addition	stepsadd.pdf
179	Taking More Steps to Add	mstepsadd.pdf

Contents of the Resource CD (cont.)

Page	Title	Filename
180	Take It Away: Subtraction Practice	takeaway.pdf
181	Follow That Symbol!	followsymbol.pdf
182	Place Value and Word Problems	placevalprob.pdf
183	More Practice with Place Value	moreplaceval.pdf
184	Finding Your Own Place	findownplace.pdf
185	Getting to the Bottom of Multiplication	getbottom.pdf
186	Multiplying Multiple Digits	multdigits2.pdf
187	Practicing Math with Equivalent Measurements	eqmeasure.pdf
188	Multiplication Body Facts	multbody.pdf
189	Multiply for Answers	multanswers.pdf
190	What's the Missing Factor?	missfactor.pdf
191	Finding Both Missing Factors	bothfactors.pdf
192	Dividing It Up	dividitup.pdf
193	What's Remaining	whatremain.pdf
194	Multiplication and Division Connection	mdconnection.pdf
195	Mystery Division Problems	mysteryprob.pdf
196	Solving Division Word Problems	solvedprob.pdf
197	Half Is Half	halfishalf.pdf
198	Making Things Equal	makeequal.pdf
199	Making Equivalent Fractions	makefrac.pdf
200	More or Less? Comparing Fractions	compfrac.pdf
201	Fraction Evaluation: Measuring Value	evalvalue.pdf
202	Writing Fraction Word Problems	wwordprob.pdf
203	Adding and Subtracting Pieces of the Pie	piecespie.pdf
204	More Than a Whole	morewhole.pdf
205	Breaking Apart a Fraction	breakfrac.pdf
206	Add Them Up!	addup.pdf
207	Mixing It Up with Mixed Numbers	mixnums.pdf
208	Adding Subtraction to the Mix	subtomix.pdf
209	Adding Mixed Numbers and Whole Numbers	mixwholenums.pdf
210	Breaking Bread: Solving Fraction Word Problems	breakbread.pdf
211	Fraction Solutions	fracsolutions.pdf
212	Improper Multiplication and Addition	improper.pdf
213	Fraction Word Problems	fractproblems.pdf
214	Keeping the Order: Multiplying Fractions	keeporderfract.pdf
215	A Fraction of a Whole Number	fracwhole.pdf
216	Real World Fractions	realfractions.pdf
217	Fraction Party Riddles	partyriddle.pdf
218	More Fraction Riddles	moreriddle.pdf
219	Fractions with Tens and Hundreds	fractenshund.pdf
220	Putting Tens and Hundreds Together	tenhundtogeth.pdf
221	Turning a Decimal Into a Fraction	turndecimal.pdf
222	Getting Decimals in Line	getline.pdf
223	Decimals Large and Small	largesmall.pdf
224	Measure It Up!	measureup.pdf
225	Relative Sizes of Measurement	sizes.pdf
226–227	Equivalent Measurements	eqmeasure.pdf
228	Solving Word Problems	solveword.pdf
229	Tick Tock Goes the Clock: Elapsed Time Problems	ticktock.pdf
230–231	Finding Perimeter: Distance Around a Space	distance.pdf
232–233	How Large Is Your Area?	largearea.pdf

Contents of the Resource CD *(cont.)*

Page	Title	Filename
234	Line Them Up: Making Line Plots	makeplots.pdf
235	Connecting the Dots: Interpreting Data on a Line Plot	connectdots.pdf
236	Circle Round: Measuring Angles	measureangles.pdf
237	Cutting Through the Circle	cutcircle.pdf
238	Using a Protractor Like a Pro	protractor.pdf
239	Sketching an Angle	sketchangle.pdf
240	180 is the Magic Number	magic.pdf
241	More Than a Simple Dot or Line	simpledotline.pdf
242	Line, Line Segment, or Ray?	linesegment.pdf
243	Drawing Perpendicular and Parallel Lines	drawperp.pdf
244	Shape Up! Identifying Shapes	idenshapes.pdf
245–246	Right Triangles and Right Angles	rightangles.pdf
247	Identifying Lines of Symmetry	identsymm.pdf
248	Symmetry or Not?	symnot.pdf

Notes

Notes

Notes

Notes

#50908—Bright & Brainy: 4th Grade Practice